KNIVES, KNIFE FIGHTING, & RELATED HASSLES

KNIVES, KNIFE FIGHTING, & RELATED HASSLES

How to Survive a REAL Knife Fight

Marc "Animal" MacYoung

PALADIN PRESS
BOULDER, COLORADO

Also by Marc "Animal" MacYoung:

Barroom Brawling (video, with Peyton Quinn)
Cheap Shots, Ambushes, and Other Lessons
Down but Not Out (video)
Fists, Wits, and a Wicked Right
Floor Fighting
Pool Cures, Beer Bottles, & Baseball Bats
Professional's Guide to Ending Violence Quickly
Safe in the City (with Chris Pfouts)
Safe in the Street (video)
Street E&E
Surviving a Street Knife Fight (video)
Taking It to the Street
Violence, Blunders, and Fractured Jaws
Winning a Street Knife Fight (video)

Knives, Knife Fighting, & Related Hassles:
How to Survive a REAL Knife Fight
by Marc "Animal" MacYoung

Copyright © 1990 by Marc "Animal" MacYoung
ISBN 10: 0-87364-544-8
ISBN 13: 978-0-87364-544-7
Printed in the United States of America

Published by Paladin Press, a division of
Paladin Enterprises, Inc.
Gunbarrel Tech Center
7077 Winchester Circle
Boulder, Colorado 80301 USA
+1.303.443.7250

Direct inquiries and/or orders to the above address.

Visit our Web site at www.paladin-press.com

This book is dedicated to my family, some of whom don't understand why I walk the Warrior's Path, but I love them anyway.

▼

Contents

Chapter One

▼

Knives and Related Hassles

Never too proud to duck...

Paul Moheny

I suddenly knew, in my heart of hearts, that something was way the fuck wrong. As I threw myself backwards, there was an arching blur of steel where my stomach had been a moment before. To this day, I can't tell you what it was that warned me; maybe it was something about the way the guy crossed his arms. I just knew it was time to go. The only thing I left behind was my macho attitude; the rest of my skinny little ass was backpedaling real quick.

As I landed about three feet away from where I had recently almost been dissected, my blade slid into my hand. The action was real easy and real smooth. I slipped into a fighting crouch and stared at the punk. He looked at me for a moment in total confusion. Several things weren't quite the same as before: 1) his surprise attack had just missed, and not because he hadn't done it right; 2) I was also armed; 3) he had never seen the fighting form I was in; 4) it was obvious by the ease and speed with which I had just gone into my fighting stance that I had done this before; and 5) if he pushed it he was either going to get seriously hurt or die.

1

Now, all of this is a guess as to what the guy was thinking based on the following action: he ran away. For about five minutes I stood there shaking from adrenaline and swearing like a sailor. Then I went off and continued what I had been doing before the punk showed up.

It's sort of pathetic, but most knife incidents end up with an exciting conclusion like that—one participant running away. The reasons are many, usually consisting of some guy realizing he's going to get hurt bad if he hangs around. Of the remaining types of knife fights or assaults, somebody gets cut anywhere from slightly to seriously, and sometimes somebody even gets killed. For the most part, these situations consist of only one guy having a knife, or less often two fools wagging knives around until somebody accidently gets cut. The final type of knife incident is where the shit gets ugly— that's two trained knife fighters going at it full on. The only way to sum up that situation is the old Chinese proverb: "When two tigers fight, one dies, the other is wounded."

Like my last book, *Cheap Shots, Ambushes, and Other Lessons,* this is not going to be a dissertation on "never-fail knife fighting forms." There are a whole messa books out there that will go into technique, training, attacks, and overall dick hardening. Merry Christmas, read them and know them. For what they are saying, they are good. Since that information is already out there though, I'm not going to waste our time repeating it.

What I am going to tell you about are realities that I have learned from hard lessons in the streets of America. These are points they don't cover in the "Green Beenie" manuals, but you will encounter if you use a knife in America. The problem, as I see it, is most other books tell you all about the "Gung Ho Kill 'Em All, Let God Sort 'Em Out" theory of knife fighting. Thing is, if you slither through the bushes sneaking up on a little brown guy with an AK-47, that's the right attitude to have about knife fighting. In a honky tonk in front of a hundred witnesses, you can get into serious trouble for that sort of approach. I mean face it, you not only have to survive the incident, you have to be able to say afterward to the authorities, "See? My dick's clean!" This is something you really have to contend with, otherwise you're going to be reading *Put 'Em Down, Take 'Em Out! Knife Fighting Techniques from Folsom Prison* in Folsom Prison. By that time it's sorta late.

Another type of knife incident is ambushes and other rude surprises that you'll encounter in bars and on the street. These come in different forms than in the bush. If you don't know what to watch out for, you're going to get cut bad without ever knowing what hit you, because *it is a different situation!*

The real trick about street knife fighting is proper judgment. That means either knowing how much it will take to get the job done without overkilling, or recognizing that the only way to survive will be by immediately going into total combat mode. To put it simply, will just pulling your own knife out and wagging it around scare the asshole enough to make him run away, or are you going to have to kill him?

In my first book I went on about the difference between fighting and combat. Guess what? SOSDB (Same Old Shit, Different Book). I'll phrase it differently so you won't get bored, though.

A fight is two people in an altercation over something. It has rules and limits. You may not think so, but it's true. Have you ever seen two guys going at it while their friends watch? The buddies are sitting around drinking beer, cheering, and just generally having a hoot. There comes a point, however, where one guy begins to lose. Bingo! We all know how this movie is going to end. Time to stop it and get back to serious drinking. It's easy—couple o' buddies walk up and drag the sluggers apart. That is a fight. You don't allow anybody to get hammered too hard. If you're in it, you keep some restraint. Punch around a bit, don't win by too much, and possibly buy the guy a beer later. This is what I joke about. Face it, fat lips heal. It ain't no big deal.

Combat, on the other hand, is about as funny as the plague. People die because of this shit. Combat is full-scale out-and-out murder and mayhem. A lot of shit goes down because people don't differentiate between fighting and combat. Two guys get into a fight and one guy freaks because he's losing. Suddenly he ups the ante by taking a serious shot at the other guy's throat. Now you're in combat, and the stone-cold minimum is somebody's going to get hurt. The worst is one guy ends up dead and the other doing hard time. That's the truth of combat in America.

When the paramilitary-macho-fucks tell you to be ready to kill at all times, they're only telling you half the story. They are talking about combat, and *in that sense they are right*. One of the main differences between a fight and combat is in combat every escape option is closed off. Your entire world is involved and at that moment nothing else matters. You are there, and you have to direct every ounce of energy into surviving.

Which brings up the difference between a combat veteran and a tough guy. The tough guy has always had the option to run away and try again later. The vet has had his ass in the meat grinder and come through anyway. Putting it another way, the vet is ready to fight for his life again if he has to. The tough guy is only fighting for his ego. A tough guy will keep on escalating it until either he wins or chickens out. It is the proverbial "gotta prove something" attitude.

Because of their unpredictability, however, tough guys are both dangerous and a pain in the ass. They really don't know when to quit because their egos won't let them. These are the guys who go to their car after they've lost a fight and get their gun or, in this case, when they start to lose, they pull a knife. They are dangerous because they think they always *have* to "win." In order to achieve this, they'll go to extremes that sane people won't. They think of nothing beyond their bruised egos and immediate vengeance.

Another subspecies of tough guy is the person who is, in all reality, just plain scared. The reason he drew his knife is because, truth be told, he simply panicked. You are so good that the poor guy thinks he is going to die, so he's going to try to hit you with everything he's got.

These guys are actually sorta easy to deal with if you have

some time and can keep your wits. Oddly enough, there's often a small pause after the weapon is drawn in these situations (especially if you've done the smart thing and back-pedaled). This can be used to your advantage. As you're drawing your knife, your real weapon is your flapping lips. Tell him the truth. You really don't want to kill him, and even if he wins he's in trouble because he pulled the knife first. The point you want to make is there is an alternative, and that is to just *go away*. Unless he jackrabbits into "macho-man mode," let him go. If you leave a way out, it's incredible the number of times people will run away.

That's what I did with the guy who tried to cut me. I didn't even have to say anything; I just stood my ground and looked *real* dangerous. He got the message; it was time to go.

These are the two basic types of toughs you'll meet out there. There are other variations, but this will give you a model to start with.

You should be able to recognize the difference between a tough guy and a combat veteran. A vet knows what it's like to have to fight for his life. For this reason, most times a vet won't want to fight at all. He'd rather be left alone because fighting isn't a game to him. A vet won't bring his ego into a fight. He won't even bring his humanity. If you fuck with a vet you won't be dealing with anything human. In fact, it's sorta questionable if what you're facing is even alive. This is the point of extreme that is created by real combat.

The weird thing about the way most people handle vets is that they freak out and think the guy is going to go A.W.O.L. on them. They think only loony-toons get that far out. It's true that some wackos are that far out, yet there's a subtle but real difference between the vibes of a vet and the vibes of a loony.

Unlike a tough, one of the things a vet knows is in combat, the guy who moves first usually wins. He also knows that if you're lucky enough to waste him, you may not win round two with the friends of the deceased. *This does happen!* You kill one of my friends and I'll come looking for you. The same thing can be said about killing me. That's why messing with this kind of person is not wise.

It's real interesting; when you have fifteen vets sitting around, nobody is really anxious to start shit. Especially in regard to knife fighting, vets are safer than toughs because shit is less likely to start over pointless things. If it does start, odds are it's going to be serious, both in cause and result.

Another thing about knives you should know is that they are preferred by people who are a little harder in spirit. It's interesting to note that in California it's a felony to carry a concealed knife and a misdemeanor to carry a concealed gun. This is indicative of the police's familiarity with knife-fighting cultures.

You see, guns attract people's attention for some reason. It's sort of hard to remove somebody quietly with a gun without expensive (and illegal) equipment. The same isn't true for knives, though. You hear a gunshot over the noise of the city; you don't hear a scuffle in the shadows.

A second aspect that makes the authorities nervous about knife fighters is that knife fighters have to be close to someone to do damage. This puts them at risk, too. In other words, to do someone with a knife you have to be serious enough to risk your ass to get them. While it's true most shootings happen at about seven feet (past that, most people can't aim for shit), knifings are generally carried out from only inches apart. This means you have to still be fighting the guy as you're killing him. It calls for a little more commitment than the average person with a gun can muster.

Another thing about knives that makes them less than popular with the police is they don't provide the extensive ballistics that guns do. Also, people are less adverse to wiping knives clean and throwing them away than they are guns. For some bozo reason, a lot of people keep the gun that they shot somebody with. Not necessarily true with knives.

The final aspect about knife fighting that makes the authorities twitchy is that because it's more dangerous to the attacker, knife fighters are usually sneakier. Ambushes, blind shots, and trick attacks are more the norm than the exception. There must be something about guns that makes inexperienced people feel invincible. They think that it's the old John Wayne shoot-out bit, with lead flying and their enemies dropping like flies. A knife fighter cannot have such delusions. Shadows and surprise are both friends and enemies to him. Real knife fighters are closer to hit men than dueling gunfighters. If you're going to carry a knife, it is really advisable to remember this if you're interested in breathing.

In my previous book I ranted and raved about awareness, world models, setups, Alpha and Beta behavior, and so on. This book is going to be more specific. In regard to awareness and such, the general outline is in *Cheap Shots, Ambushes, and Other Lessons* (hint, hint, nudge, nudge, blatant plug, blatant plug).

What I *am* going to repeat is that this book, like the first one, is not a bible. I don't know everything there is to know about knife fighting, but neither does anybody else. The information in this book comes from my own personal experiences and observations that have led to certain conclusions. The fact that I'm still breathing indicates that there's at least some truth to these conclusions.

I'm not saying now, nor will I ever say that this book provides absolute laws. Rather, it is a rough outline that you can apply to the way you see the world in hopes of making it work better for you. So if something in this book doesn't work for you, 10-22 it! Go out and discover what works for you, because in the end, that's the only way to really learn anything.

Staying alive is a never-ending process that you always have to correct and readjust to get it to work right. Life, when it works, is pure joy, but if you don't take care of it, it'll turn into a real bitch until you just end up leaving it (very much like a Harley ergo the line, "Life is like a Harley").

While we're at it, this book is predicated on the assumption that you've read my last one and understood some of the concepts and slang I use. Also, I hope that you're aware of the fact that I'd fuck around at my own funeral. So, "Hi ho, hi ho, it's off to learn about knife fighting we go!"

Chapter Two

Nuts and Bolts

Why dance at all when you can fuck 'em in the dark?
Me (holding up a knife).

Knives are like sex; it's really a matter of personal preference as to what turns you on. There are big ones, little ones, fat ones, and thin ones. Some are for work and some are for play. Some feel great and others just don't ever feel quite right. Some are old friends, and others are pretty but just passing acquaintances. (Guys, back me up on this one. I didn't say "women" once, did I? If some women's libber comes after me, I got witnesses!)

Anyway, now that I've protected myself, back to knives. There are two basic types of short-bladed objects: one is called a *dagger* and the other is called a *knife*. The difference is that a dagger is a *double-edged weapon*, while a knife is a *single-edged tool*. Now if you really want to get complicated, there's a borderland between the two, often referred to as a "dirk," which is a blade with one full edge and up to half the length of the other side edged. In this book, I'm just going to call everything a knife and fuck the linguistics.

Before you go out and drop some money into a fighting knife, check your state and municipal ordinances as to what you can legally have and carry (the two not being synonymous). You can find out about the state ordinances by hitting the local library and looking them up. The municipality, however, calls for a little more work.

Step one: Don't walk into the police station and ask about knives. If you go waltzing into a police station or ask a cop on the street, they're going to be a little curious about what you're up to. Instead, go to city hall and ask to see the municipal codes. And for God's sake, don't give them your name!

When you're there, look up every word you can think of for different types of knives. It's a safe bet that not all of the laws were written at the same time, which means they are going to be scattered around throughout the codes. Since we all know that the sole purpose of lawyers is to make money by confusing the issue, you'll know to look under many different headings. Daggers are covered in one area, folding knives in another, locking somewhere else, concealed in a totally different neck of the woods, and gravity blades somewhere else altogether. Also, check to see if there are laws prohibiting the carrying rather than the owning of a particular type of knife. While we're being paranoid, check into the laws about having one when you drive.

The reason I'm telling you all of this is if you carry a knife, you *will* get checked out sooner or later by the cops. Cops don't like knife fighters because they really are more dangerous than the average citizen with a gun. When you wear a knife, especially at the belt, you are letting people know that you are serious. Now, you may only be serious about not becoming a victim, but the cops don't know that. That's because they think nice people don't carry knives. Nice people get mugged, robbed, and killed because they politely wait for the police to show up and take the nasty person to jail. Unfortunately, most police officers are busy writing bullshit tickets because the mayor wants to raise funds to pay for all the deadbeats who loaf at city hall and call it work (snarl).

Now and then, the cops get a chance to get away from

writing tickets to go chase some bad guys. The thing is, when they catch the bad guys and put them in jail, the system has come up with cockamamy ways to put them back on the streets. The cops have to spend most of their time chasing down chickenshit violations that make the city and state money, while the serious but less lucrative shit is moving through a revolving door. Sometimes the best the cops can do is find the most serious type of potential trouble and check it out. If you carry a knife, you are classified as potential trouble.

Daggers are the real hot debate. A knife is a tool that can be used as a weapon, but a dagger is a stone-cold weapon. Its sole purpose is to carve people into little ribbons. While you can use a dagger as a tool, its design seriously limits its usefulness as such because of the lack of leverage by thumb application. I carried a dagger for years until I just got fed up with hassles from the cops.

While daggers are technically legal in California, the penal code statutes are phrased in such a way that the authorities can bust you if they want. It happened to my brother, "Kaos." It was a bullshit bust and they knew it, but they needed something to get him into the system. He eventually beat it, but at the cost of both time and money. I got away with it because I used to be able to recite code and verse at them. I once knew a biker on Hollywood Boulevard who carried a penal code book with him at all times just for that reason.

So be warned. If you decide to carry a dagger, be ready to back it up with your mouth and knowledge as well as everything else. From personal experience I can tell you that the most effective way to deal with the police is calmly and rationally. Don't get flamed or righteous about being stopped; it'll just turn ugly and believe me, cops know how to deal with ugly real well. If you simply state the laws and remain a quiet, well-mannered, and responsible citizen who is not going to wig out and start carving up little old ladies, they are more likely to accept the fact that you carry a knife. They still won't like it, but they're more likely to accept it.

Another thing that catches a cop's eye is a big knife. If you wander around with a pig sticker hanging to your knee, don't even think of asking me why there's cops thicker than flies on shit all over you. While it is a matter of personal choice and physical build, I personally don't like big knives, especially in the city. Now, I'm an old bush popper from way back. When I get fed up with the city, I split into the bush for a while. I admit, there I use a big survival knife. Actually, I use my normal knife, a survival knife, and a hatchet in tandem. (If you're telling yourself I should only need one good survival knife to make it, ever lost your knife out there? I have. That's why I have backups.)

A big knife is not really something you want to flaunt in the city. Also, unless you're a gorilla, a smaller knife is faster on the average, and, as you'll soon see, speed is *real* important in a knife fight. It will make you think twice about carrying an Arkansas toothpick if you know that it can sometimes take up to a second longer to draw and get into position. Now maybe one second doesn't sound all that long, but wait until you read the quick-draw chapter before you make any decisions. The counter to this whole point is that a heavy knife makes a hell of a yawara stick/brass knuckle combo, so it really is personal choice and your particular fighting style.

Now, I like to fish. It's a great way to justify hanging out, doing nothing, and drinking beer in the sunshine. In the fishing world, though, there are these things called *lures*. A lure's primary function is to catch fish. Failing at that, its secondary function is to catch fishermen. I am amazed at the number of guys who buy pretty but totally useless lures with the same rapture that a bird has when it sees a "sparkly." The same can be said for knives, but instead it's "sharpie!"

There are a number of knives that are just out-and-out wicked looking. I mean, these things are something to drool over: swept back lines, wickedly curved beveled back edge, delicious lines on the handle, and all that. Some of them are good. Lots of them are shit. What makes a good knife is the quality of steel, construction, balance, heft, and grip, not how it looks.

Before you go rushing out to buy a knife, shop for a while. Don't buy one until you've played with at least ten or twenty. If a gun or knife show is happening in your neck of the woods, go there and shop. (You can get a better deal there than in a cutlery or surplus store.)

With all knives, the grade of the steel is of utmost importance. The higher the grade, the harder the steel. Harder steel can hold a razor edge for a longer time. But there are a couple of drawbacks. One is that the higher the grade of steel, the more brittle it is. (There are certain exceptions to this, but unless you can drop $200 for a knife, it's a pretty good rule of thumb.) That means if you hit something hard with it, you can have some problems. Incidentally, don't ever hit two hammer heads together; they literally explode. Exploding hammers mean flying shrapnel, in case you didn't guess. This is what I mean by brittle. They are so strong that they won't bend, they'll break. The other thing about high-grade steel is that while they hold an edge much longer, they are a real bitch for the beginner to sharpen. You can get a decent middle-grade knife that is relatively easy to sharpen for reasonable money.

Going down the grades, you get into shitty steel pretty quickly. Crappy steel from Mexico, the Philippines, and Japan is basically a waste of time. While a better grade of steel will lose its edge by use, the cheap stuff will dull by rubbing in its sheath and just being exposed to air. A common trick is to chrome or matte-black cheap blades. This is done to hide the fact that the metal is about a half step above aluminum. Since most of the steel is cheap, the chrome job is too. If you learn to see the difference between steel and chrome, you can avoid getting ripped off. It's hard to describe, but chrome feels...well...shallow.

The next great debate is over folding, locking, straight, fixed, spring, and gravity knives. Okay, off we go into descriptions again. A folding knife is any blade that folds into its handle/sheath: jackknives, pen knives, Swiss Army knives, and so on. Truth is, you don't want to use one of these in a knife fight because it doesn't lock into an open position. One strike at the back of your hand and your knife folds up and cuts your finger. (Yes, I just told you what to do if someone ever pulls one on you.)

Locking knives are folding blades that lock into place. Some municipalities have tried to make it illegal to carry them, so check with your local regs. I've seen a guy busted because he was carrying a Buck knife in its sheath. They tried to nail him on both a locking/gravity and concealed-weapon violation. Chickenshit bust and he beat it, but it happened. (In fact, in Los Angeles about ten years ago, the cops' hassling people about knives got so out of hand that I knew a few guys who started wearing clear plastic sheaths so the cops couldn't claim their knives were concealed.)

I know a lot of guys who are good at getting their folding knives out in the open real quick. While I personally prefer fixed blades, there's a valid argument for both. The best one for folding/locking knives that I have heard is that people are less freaked out by them than fixed blades. Now at first, you may want to swagger around and scare the taxpayers by having a knife at your belt, but to tell you the truth, after a while it gets a little stale. Then it heads directly into pain-in-the-ass status. I have seen people wig out more about the three-inch fixed blade at my side than the eight-inch monster folder that the guy next to me was carrying. Anyway, the big advantage about having a folder is that people are less likely to treat you like you're a relative of Vlad the Impaler.

Gravity and spring knives are next, which includes switch-blades, stilettos, wheel locks, and balisongs (also known as butterfly knives). If you really insist on being flashy, there ain't nothing better than these babies. You whip one of these suckers out in a crowd of civilians, look sly, smooth, and bad as you flash it around, and you'll hear assholes slam shut for twenty feet around. I mean, if you're out to impress people there is nothing better. Don't try to impress a serious knife fighter this way though, because while you're showing off, he'll step in and make you eat it.

Gravity and spring knives are really a matter of personal taste. I've seen good ones in my travels, but I gotta admit, most of what gets to us is pure shit. They break, dull, wobble, and bind at the worst times. When I was a kid I used to carry a switchblade. (I was from the wrong side of the tracks, remember?) I got in a hassle with some other kids and I bravely pulled out my blade. To be honest, I had been playing with it a lot and the spring was a little tired. It had acted up before. So when I pushed the button expecting the sinister click, the blade fell out of its groove and sort of swung there like a limp dick in the wind. They took my knife away and beat me up. It was real embarrassing.

The point is, if you're going to carry this sort of flashy equipment, do yourself a favor and get a good one. You should also know that with all types of fold-up weapons, you run the risk of never getting the sucker out in time, especially if you're up against someone with experience. The guy will see the move toward your weapon and it'll be over. So watch yourself.

Now let's talk about something that is really serious—blade sharpening. I'm not going to go into it except to say that you should always have your blade paper-slicing sharp. No shit, no lie. I once got in a knife fight where the guy's blade took me across the arm. It was so dull that it didn't cut skin. I couldn't believe it. I stopped and looked at it in confusion for a second because I wasn't bleeding. Then I couldn't help myself—I started laughing at him. The guy was basically trying to fight with a butter knife. So the sharpness of your blade is something you should really be concerned about. I know about eight different ways to sharpen knives, but I'll let someone like "Ragnorak" or "Avatar" write about it. I'll go get laid instead.

Chapter Three

▼

Mental Homework

When I saw that he doubted everything, I concluded that I knew as much as he did, and that I didn't need anyone's help to be ignorant.

Voltaire

When a knife flashes past your face, it is prone to catch your attention. In fact, it could be considered an indication that you haven't covered every base as tightly as you should. Since a knife fight is a speeded-up version of a regular fight, those old basics come into play. The first thing we're going to go over is what happens leading up to a knife fight. This is probably the most important aspect of your self-defense formula.

Defense is the overview of everything you do to stay alive 'till it's time to pick up your paycheck. *Guard* is what you do when you're in the shit. So guard is an immediate manifestation of defense, but defense is the big Kahuna. That's why we're going to deal with them separately.

The major part of defense is...guess what? Right! Awareness! Very good, you get a cookie! Yes, boys and girls, awareness has come back to haunt you. So let's look at some specifics of awareness as applied to knife fighting.

Premise one: You don't want to get stabbed; it would be bad. Premise two: It is harder not to get stabbed when your opponent has already pulled his knife. Conclusion: prevent him from pulling it out by hook or by crook.

Let's assume that you're sitting in your favorite bar unwinding after a rough day at work. It's cool; you're known there and it's friendly. So you're sipping a beer, minding your own business, and some lithesome young hardbelly is looking at you with an interested gleam in her eye. Out of nowhere some whip-dick tough guy comes up and starts giving you trouble. Well, you got a knife on your side. Thing is, so does he. How are you going to play this?

You know that when knives are pulled it can get ugly. The yo-yo seems to have no concept of the ramifications of a knife fight. Hospital, possible permanent injury/crippling, prison, or the morgue—all those fun things. There are several options. Believe it or not, the best one is to call over the bartender, point to the guy, and say, "Hey, he's hassling me." The bartender and the bouncers throw the guy out. You go back to your beer and the sweet young thing.

In a crowded situation, call in outside help if possible. If there are no reinforcements, you still have a few choices. One is to leave. Fighting is bad enough, but when knives are involved you want to do everything you can to avoid it. (In case you're thinking I've wimped out, don't. I've got something up my sleeve.) Attract the barmaid or bartender (or whoever else is around) and tell them you're leaving rather than fighting this guy. If the guy follows you out into the parking lot, he can't claim it was self-defense but you can. Get it?

You can suggest that if he really wants to fight, both of you should take off your knives and hand them to third parties. Or, my favorite: tell him you really don't want to fight. Besides being irrational, he's armed, and that makes it too much of a hassle because of cops and such. Therefore, he should go away. If he makes a move after you've announced this to the audience, even if it's without a knife, hit him with your beer bottle. Or you can break his knee cap and leave him there. He's probably expecting you to go for your knife instead of using PIBU. (My particular fighting style. It stands for a Pitcher of Bud. Either we're going to sit down and drink it together, or I'm gonna brain the fucker with it. After all, youth and skill will always be overcome by old age and treachery. When they're young, they're short on experience but long on testosterone. It clouds their thinking.) The point is, you can do all sorts of things without ever going for your knife.

The main thing to do is always keep your cool, especially when knives are involved. We are talking long-term bad news if you lose it. Especially with knives, calling in cooler heads will prevent anyone from going to jail or the hospital.

In case you hadn't noticed, I don't advocate pulling knives in front of witnesses. It leads to a thing called "hard time." This is when they put you, for long periods of time, in places with big hairy guys who have tattoos in strange places and some weird sexual tendencies. If you absolutely can't talk a knife-wielding opponent out of it, and you can't run, bluff the guy, or sucker punch him somehow, then you should consider fighting him knife to knife. Only as a last resort, though, and only after you have made every other effort. Then, if you can, nick him once and step back. At the moment of realization, when he's shocked about getting cut, tell him you could do it again, and he should back off. In fact, if you're sincere and say, "Please, I don't want to hurt you. Go away," he will take that and the sight of his own blood as a good excuse to leave. If he still comes at you after all of that, it's combat.

Most of what I have just told you is for the witnesses. If everybody confirms that you tried to escape, talk your way out of it, avoid it, and not antagonize the corpse, it's more likely to be cool. The cops call it self-defense, and you can still drive past San Quentin instead of changing your address to its mailroom.

Always remember that people will either get hurt or killed with weapons. If you survive the fight, you will have the authorities to contend with. If you kill somebody in a knife fight without covering your ass beforehand, you're going to get a chance to get in more combat situations, but this time in the prison yard. That is why part of your defense should be to plan for surviving beyond the immediate situation.

What I have just described is an example of a fight escalating into combat. There was a lot of time before the situation deteriorated to the point where somebody got hurt. It's up to you to take advantage of that time and maneuver before you have to give the guy an appendectomy.

Especially with knives, your first option should be to get help from outside sources. Aside from reasons already mentioned, it diffuses the guy's anger in other directions. If he's just a punk, he'll back down from a bouncer. If he's really a section eight, well, I've never met a bouncer who didn't have a few nasty tricks up his sleeve (like a derringer). Technically speaking, it is the bouncer's job to prevent this sort of shit from happening. The second thing you should do is leave. No judge in his right mind is going to believe that you were waiting in ambush for the guy thirty seconds after you've announced you don't want to mess with him. You leaving and him following means only one thing: self-defense. If he's with friends, call the bartender's attention to them and tell him what just happened and that you are leaving. Ask the bartender (or bouncer) to slow them down long enough for you to get out of there. Then lay low for a while.

It has been my experience that the major aggressors in life are the egotistical loony-toons who don't know when to quit. In many ways it's easier to split and not hassle with their weak egos. Don't worry; sooner or later they're going to cross the wrong person and get dropped in the ground for not knowing when to quit. If at all possible, do yourself a favor and don't be the one who does society a favor. Somebody looking for a fight isn't the same as an attack on you, so you really don't have to bite into his shit. The best way not to do that is to leave.

The next situation is when you and some yutz get in a jam in a place that is either near your home or one that you frequent. People pull you apart before it's really over. Often-times it's not settled to the guy's satisfaction. So guess who comes back for a rematch? (This sort of situation is stupid but it happens *a lot!*) Okay, he pushes it and you fight. You win and he stumps off, his little duck feelings hurt. If the guy came back at you once, it should be taken as an indication of a serious flaw in his personality. It's a hard call to make if he'll back up on you or not because it depends on a whole lot of little circumstances that are hard to explain.

It will behoove you, therefore, to cover your ass. Assume that the guy will be waiting for a chance to strike back at you, and this time he is going to up the ante. Go to Code Yellow status for about a month. This means to look both ways as you walk through doorways and don't turn your back toward entryways in restaurants, Laundromats, and those sorts of places. Check shadows as you walk down the street, and if you must carry things, carry them in your left hand, leaving your weapon hand free. Watch for cars driving slowly toward you with the passenger window open. If the putz tries to surprise you, you'll be ready.

Your behavior when you're at Code Yellow status will help cover your ass in another way. In order to get a jump on you, the guy has to watch you and figure out your pattern. After all, if he doesn't use surprise, he knows he'll get his ass kicked again. Since he wants to prove that he's better than you, he'll try to use brains instead of brawn. Bad news for him. The fact that you're reading this book is a good indication that you have a little more in the gray cell department than him. The point is, if he's watching you while you're checking shadows, he'll realize that you're a harder nut to crack than he thought. This will seriously slow him down. You see, fractured ego or not, most of these guys aren't going to want to risk their dicks again. They know that if they strike at this level and it doesn't work, they can't expect anyone to save their ass. Even if it's not a planned ambush and the guy happens to see you on a fluke and tries to come after you, you'll be able to spot him a mile away if you're alert.

The other kind of situation that happens is real simple. You've scared the shit out of some guy. The dude may have started it, but if you come on full-bore combat mode, he's going to panic, pull a knife, and stick your ass to save his own. This is why I advocate being calm when confronted with violence. I don't care how scared you are, remember the guy you're facing is probably about to wet his pants too. If it's a misunderstanding, the guy you're up against probably feels that if he isn't as strong as you, you're gonna beat him up. This is especially true if you're bigger. This is why I advocate being cool; you can avoid a lot of shit by knowing when to push and when not to.

Let's talk about height. If you're about six feet or more, the other guy may realize that he's still tall enough to kick you in the balls. If this is the case, he may feel that he has to prove that he's not afraid of you. This is something I have seen happen a number of times, and the worst offenders are not necessarily "little guys." In fact, the worst cases of "short-man-itis" I have seen have come from dudes of average height.

Height is and isn't your ally in a knife fight. Number one: if you're a big guy and you're used to overpowering everyone, you're about to encounter your first earthquake. A friend of mine got his degree in psychology doing a study of who has the hardest time dealing with earthquakes. For those of you not of Californian persuasion, when an earthquake hits there ain't shit you can do about it. The best you can do is get to a semi-safe spot and ride it out, watching the ceiling for cracks (which way the roof falls determines which way you jack rabbit).

It turned out that big guys are most likely to freak out during an earthquake. For a space of time, the only thing he can do is run away and hide, and even that might not work. This goes against the way a big man thinks. All his life he's had a fall-back position of "if all else fails, grab and overpower your opposition." In an earthquake, he is the one being grabbed and overpowered, and *all* of his strength and size is useless. The point I'm trying to make is that your first knife fight is like your first earthquake, and a blind, head-down bull rush to overpower your opponent is synonymous with death.

One good point about being big is that it extends your reach. The bad part is that a longer reach makes your arms likely targets for counterstrikes. Another good point is you can keep the guy at a distance. A bad point is that if the guy who closes with you knows street wrestling, he can turn your large size against you. A third good point about being big is you can probably take some damage before it affects you. The bad point is that you have to cover a lot more area that can be damaged. Yet another good point is you can probably grab the guy and hold him while you hurt him. The bad point is if you do it wrong, it's suicide.

In case you haven't caught on by now, no matter what size you are, you have to *think* in a knife fight. You have to rely on your wits, mobility, speed, and knowledge of the situation, not on an overwhelming belief in your physical attributes. Mistakes based on ego and pride are lethal in this business.

Come to think of it, let's talk about ego for a minute. Actually, if you want to get persnickity about it, we can call it pride. Remember I told you earlier that a combat veteran won't bring his ego into a fight? This is what I'm going to talk about. Some women have PMS (Pre-Menstrual Syndrome), which means for about one week a month they are bitchy, pushy, irrational, stupid, and irritable. Men don't have this cycle problem since they are free from a monthly biological cycle system. Instead they suffer MPS (Male-Pride Syndrome), which makes them bitchy, pushy, irrational, stupid, and irritable all the time.

Ego/pride will get you into more shit than anything else. It's weird, but you can tell when a guy's dick is doing his thinking. He'll get this glazed-over hungry look. He'll also tell you straight out that he knows what he's doing. What he's really doing is disregarding everything else while trying to get into some chick's pants. Even though the one-eyed trouser snake is doing the thinking, he'll swear up and down that he's being rational and realistic. Everybody else knows differently, though.

Well, when men are in the grip of MPS, it's just like when their dick is doing the thinking for them. The guy will swear up and down that he's being realistic and rational about taking on the Hell's Angels in a toe-to-toe slug out. People who aren't caught in the grip of MPS realize that is probably one of the best ways ever invented to commit suicide, followed closely by skinny dipping in a school of hungry piranha.

Men in the throes of MPS are often referred to as "cockstrong." They think they can whip out their super dick and beat Godzilla to death with it. One of the best ways to spot somebody who is in the middle of "that time of life" is that they think anything that isn't straight out, head-to-head, toe-to-toe brawling is either chickenshit or wouldn't work on them. (This comes from having a big red "S" tattooed on their dick. The dick of steel, able to stop bullets!) Watch people for a while and you'll see what I mean about this shit. It's true. A guy with MPS thinks that only sissies decline to fight or walk away from one. What's worse is that they think if they walk away from a fight, everybody will think that (gasp in horror) *they're sissies!* No big red "S" for sissies. Only manly men get one.

The bitch about MPS is it isn't consistent. Some guys are forever stuck in it. (Remember the guys who keep coming back at you again and again?) At other times this inconsistency can be used to your advantage. You see, MPS has this really nasty habit of suddenly, without warning, splitting. I mean, it'll take you right to the brink of a fight and all of a sudden "Bammo!" it leaves. I've seen it happen to the extreme of where it's like a switch being turned off. You can almost *see* the guy's rational mind coming back into control. One second he's ready to climb up some gorilla's leg and chew the ape's kneecap off; the next his rational mind is screaming at him, "What the fuck are you doing?!!" Meanwhile, the gorilla is winding up to start pounding him.

When MPS splits and leaves somebody in a lurch, that's the best time to let the dude go. Let him know you're not going to attack him and that if he leaves now, there's no hard feelings. You'll let it slide 'cause you understand. MPS is one of the dumbest reasons to die, but it's the most common one I know of in this kind of situation.

Up to this point I've been talking about MPS as if a third

party is suffering it. Let's talk about you. You need to be able to spot when you're in the middle of it. A good warning sign is when you feel you can't back down. Truth be told, there are very few situations when you really *have* to fight. Usually violence is used by people who either think they have no other option, or have grown lazy and think that it can solve any problem. The purpose of this chapter is to show you how many options you actually do have before you have to pull a knife.

All you really have to do is expand your concept of defense. This can and does entail getting the fuck out of someplace, or at least retreating into a better strategic position. Don't fight a guy in a place where you are in a weaker position. I don't remember who said it, but some guy who won a war of two once said, "The way to march a thousand miles and win a battle is to have the other side do the marching." If you suffer MPS, you can be led all over the place by someone who knows what he's doing or, even worse, the guy will come in from left field through any one of the five-million blind-spots that MPS creates and take your ass out. If you want to be a tough guy, go play with your dick and be proud of your MPS. If you want to live long enough to lie to your grandkids, keep your pride on a leash.

The reason I've ranted and raved throughout this chapter is to give you an idea of how serious knife fighting is. It is a dangerous and legally complicated situation to be in. It is no place for cockstrong gung-ho punks; they're weeded out real quick. When you approach the subject of knife fighting, your spirit and attitude must be of a grim professional who knows he's flying into the shit. If you're going to survive knife fighting, you must be aware of the odds, pitfalls, ramifications, and everything else.

Chapter Four

▼

Mobility and Balance

RUN!

> Dan Huebner, to me, when he noticed
> seven or eight dudes of obvious
> ill intent running after us.

Most of the time I've spent in knife fights has been in retreat. If you intend to have a long and illustrious career in the exciting field of knife fighting, you should make this a major portion of both your training and overall defense scheme. If this sticks in your craw, go back and reread the previous chapters. If that doesn't work, do the world a favor, go see a psychiatrist or, if you want to save money, suck a bullet out of a gun, because you're probably suicidal or have terminal MPS (which is the same thing in the long run).

Mobility and balance are two of the most critical aspects of knife fighting, the reason being that if you know how to use them, you are more in control of what's happening. In knife combat the odds are you're going to have to close with the guy at some point. If you are mobile and in balance, you can pretty much choose *when* you will close with him. In other words, when you close with him will be your choice, not his.

If you're not in balance when you move, you won't be able to react in time if something goes wrong. For example, if

27

you lunge way the fuck out there and something goes wrong, what are your options? Let's say that the guy stepped to the right of your lunge and is stabbing under your arm at your gut. If your left arm is acting as a counterbalance and you move it to block his stab, you might succeed. If you can't get out of it fast enough, the combo of losing your counterbalance and the added impact of blocking will stall your energy and gravity will take over. Either you'll fall (definitely uncool), or while you're busy hopping around like a one-legged chicken trying to regain your balance, he'll attack again. This time you may not be so lucky—he might attack you in such a way that you can't block without falling over, like slashing at your kidney or shoulder.

Another way the movie could play is when you shift your body out of the way of the stab. Do it wrong and you're like Rover—about to roll over and play dead. Don't think the guy is going to wait for you to get up. He'll probably land on you with his knife going stabbity-stab.

The third situation is when you plain just get stuck because

You don't need a Ph.D. to see that this guy is way off balance. You could easily knock him over. If you were to slip his attack, you could have your pick of many targets. Without getting fancy, figure out how many ways you could take out someone who's this far off balance.

you couldn't do anything in time. The fourth and worst possibility is when he not only stabs you but closes with you as well. He's bound your right arm against you with his body. His left arm snakes around your neck and shoulders, keeping you from rolling away. The added impact and weight has totally fucked your balance, you're falling, and he's riding you to the ground. While all of this is happening he's doing needlepoint on your guts.

That less-than-pleasant description is what can and will happen in a knife fight if you attack unbalanced. Now let's replay the movie but with you in balance when you attack. You can put on your little white hat, too, if you want. An attack that is in balance never really gets too far past the outer perimeter of your guard, which means if something goes wrong you can get back home real quick. Let's say you lunge and the guy slips your attack (moves to one side). Because you're in balance, you can block and change your direction all at once (like immediately) without having to worry about gravity complicating your life.

This is a balanced attack. Even with the beer belly, if something were to go wrong it's still possible to change directions immediately. Someone successfully slipping this stance runs the risk of anything from an elbow in the throat to a kick in the balls.

An unbalanced person cannot react fast enough to the con-
tinually changing circumstances of a knife fight. The body's
weight and velocity have to be stopped, caught up with, their
direction changed and then the weight has to be restarted
into motion. Now, all fancy physics formulas aside, that
translates into one thing: lost time before you can do
something else. In a knife fight, lost time translates into leak-
ing holes in your body.

A balanced person can actually redirect his energy. No
stopping, stalling, restarting, and all that. He just suddenly
goes another way and all parts follow at the same speed, even
if the new direction is 180° from the previous course. This
is why balance is important to mobility.

Another good thing about being balanced is that if your
footing is unsure, you are less likely to have your feet slip
out from under you. Slick or wet floors, ice, or floors with
dirt and/or sawdust are surfaces you may have to fight on
(that's why you should practice on them). If you're in balance,
you won't slip because you're pressing directly down into
the ground. When you're not in balance, you're really pushing
down at an angle, which cuts down on solid traction.

You might study a martial art form and have pretty good
balance during your katas. But here's a little test you can do
at home. Turn up the stereo and dance around the room.
The trick is to keep in balance at all times. No cheating; you
can't fall into kata. You have to make the steps up as you
go along.

If you don't feel that unbalanced wobble in your pelvic
area more than twice during a long song, you're doing pretty good. If you do feel it more than twice, it's time for the
old "walk-the-railroad-tracks" type of training to perfect your
balance during motion. After you have the straight forward
part down, it's time to do side-to-side, then circles, and so
on. The reason I suggest this is that with all of my martial
arts training, I've seldom, if ever, found myself in a perfect
kata position during a fight. (By the way, when working on
your balance, keeping the knees bent is one of the major
secrets to getting it right.)

Okay, on to mobility. Hey, guess what? I sure hope you haven't turned your stereo down, 'cause it's dance time again. Boogaloo until you puke! In the middle of the room, begin to move around in circles (remembering your balance!). As you change directions, imagine a blow coming in from that sector. Now dodge it. Don't block, dodge, until you get to the point where you can change directions immediately from any angle.

The next step is to pick a point in the room. Your imaginary opponent is there. All the attacks originate from that point. (Fortunately, somebody nailed his foot to the floor so he can't move too far from there.) Skip around dodging ghost lunges for a while until you either get the hang of it or get bored (hopefully it's the hang of it part).

Now the game gets a little more complicated. Instead of stabs he's slashing at you. A slash takes up a level, which makes it important to decide if it's a long slash or a short one. If it's a short slash (done just to nick you and make you geek so something else can be snaked in), you can sometimes chicken neck it out of the way (geeking is optional). If it's a long slash (a slash designed to cut deep), practice immediate backpedaling.

Now, here comes one of my famous exceptions to the rules. Sometime during a knife fight (and to a lesser degree, regular fighting), you're going to have to sacrifice balance for getting the fuck out of there quick, especially when long slashes are involved. What I meant by a slash "taking up a level" is simple. Think of your face, your stomach, and your dick. A slash at any of those levels means that you want to very quickly remove your anatomy at that particular level outside the slash range. If you're in balance to begin with, you can do this with relative ease. Then, your little feet come running to catch up with your rapidly retreating stomach. As long as you are far enough out of attack range to regain it when you finish backpedaling, this is a time when you can disregard balance. But remember, *don't ever lose balance while initiating an attack.*

Now comes a new game. Your imaginary opponent has just

pulled his foot free of the floor. EEEK! Like a shark he's circling, waiting for a chance to strike. Hah! He pounces. You dodge! Again and again this goes on while you learn how to dodge. Finally, you get tired of dodging and pull out an imaginary gun and blow ol' numb nuts away. Isn't imagination a wonderful thing?

What you were doing there with your little buddy was training your body to react and retain balance during semi-random circumstances. After you get the hang of doing this with imaginary opponents, it's time for the next step—a real friend with a rubber knife. I suggest getting rubber knives from a martial art supply store since they're more prone to be realistically weighted. If there isn't a martial art store nearby, try a toy store. If the clerk looks at you funny, mumble something about your nephew wanting them. If all else fails, go get those dinky little plastic ones that supermarkets or drug stores usually have on their toy rack.

The reason I advocate rubber knives instead of sticks or cardboard knives is that you are training your body to react to a certain set of cues. It's easier to imagine that a rubber knife is a real knife than it is to imagine that a stick is a fake knife, much less a real one. The reason I don't advocate using real knives is because you are about to discover how unpredictable knife fighting is. I'd like to keep the bleeding down to a minimum.

You now have your little toy knives. On to training. The rub is you don't get to have one yet. Your friend does, though. He gets to chase you around trying to stick, poke, stab, slash, and generally harass you. You get to run away a lot. No blocking yet, just avoidance. Take turns chasing each other around until you get good enough not to get stabbed too often.

It is important to get this particular aspect down real well before you go on to other ones. Once you get into the habit of not standing there and taking unnecessary punishment, you have the right attitude.

Chapter Five

▼

Guard

The bravest are surely those who have the clearest vision of what is before them, glory and danger alike, and yet not withstanding go out and meet it.

Thucydides

Guard is real easy to define. It's what you do to prevent your ass from getting poked. Your guard should cover the space around, above, and below you that you can easily protect. Some people like to extend it out a little. If they can do it, fine. (Sorry, a Smith and Wesson doesn't count as an extended guard.)

When something enters your guard area, you should try to stop it at the perimeter. This can be somewhat of a bitch in a knife fight though, because what's entering that area is the sharp part. It makes things messy if you hit it wrong. Despite this problem, you still have to try to block, counter, or dodge an incoming knife, depending on which way it's coming in.

Now, if you've done your homework from the previous chapter and practiced scuttling around to avoid getting poked, you're probably pretty good at ducking. Now you get to add blocks. You still don't get a knife yet; that comes later.

Since knife fighting usually relies on speed rather than strength, the most effective types of blocks are the slap/whip kind. These are blocks that originate from the wrist, using the elbow as a pivot point. One way of looking at them is, under control, you throw your wrist at an incoming strike. When done properly, the wrist will arrive at the destination the moment your arm's motion is arrested. This allows for all of the energy to be transferred into whatever is hit. Look at the photos and see if you can figure out what I mean. Then wander over to a table or a wall and practice blocking this way. It's incredible the amount of energy transmitted by that simple wrist action, ain't it?

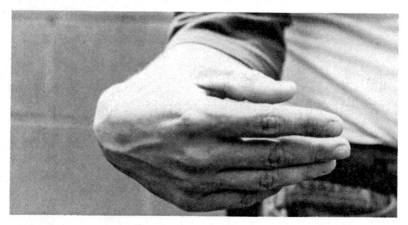

Slap block (right guard).

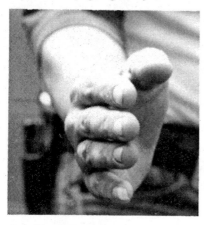

Slap block (middle or starting position).

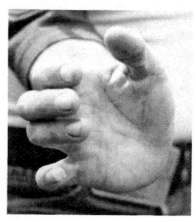

Slap block (left guard).

Slap/whip blocks are fantastic to have in your arsenal. You need to seriously practice to get the accuracy and timing down pat. In time you'll become lightning quick because for the most part they are done with a semi-relaxed arm, which means the mothers are fast. They are much faster than karate blocks. (Karate blocks use the entire length of your forearm. Since more area is involved, you can be sloppier with karate blocks than you can with slap/whip blocks. This does not necessarily work to your advantage, however, because you lose speed and accuracy.)

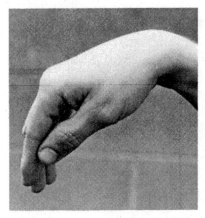 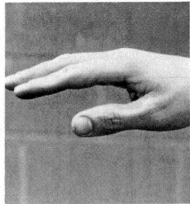

Whip block (top, or up whip)   **Whip block (middle or starting position).**

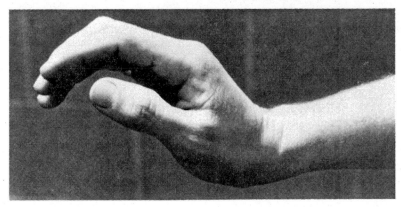

Whip block (bottom, or downward whip).

How and where to counterstrike a knife attack depends on the direction of the attack. One side of a knife, the edge, is dangerous, while the back of a knife isn't and therefore can be struck by a block. (See why daggers have the double edge? There are other reasons.) Low stabs can be slapped down because of this, as can some short slashes. But watch out here. If you're up against an experienced knife fighter, it could be a setup—done intentionally slow so when you take the bait he can speed up and point rip you (or worse).

There is all sorts of stuff written about shifting knife grips in a fight. I'll go into that later. What I want to get into right now is shifting edge direction. There are certain grips that allow for more flexibility regarding which way the edge is pointing. The best of these have to do with a wider range of wrist movement. When you are up against someone with a more flexible type of grip, your blocks should reflect that little fact. A good knife fighter works for the most part from the wrist and elbow. If you block an attack by someone who is using a flexible grip, unless you can immobilize the wrist immediately, get out of there! With a flip of the wrist he can slash you big time. If the guy is an experienced fighter he'll know that little tidbit. On blocks, unless you're going in for the kill, get out as fast as you got in. If you are going in for the kill, you want to grab his knife hand to keep him from counterstriking.

One important thing about slap/whip blocks is that they allow you to keep your hands open. This deluxe feature allows you to grab the opponent's knife hand if the opportunity presents itself. That ought to slow him down enough to allow you to whittle in relative safety for a second or two. Think about it.

Finally, a major aspect of guard is knowing what parts you *don't* want to get cut off. Most of these will be covered in the targeting chapter, but you should know up front that certain areas are choice targets. Many of these can be protected by the stance you choose. When you choose a stance, however, certain target areas will most likely be attacked. Your guard should adjust accordingly to protect these areas.

Chapter Six

▼

Grip, Heft, and Balance

*A man cannot escape the force of action by abstaining from
actions: he does not attain success just by renunciation.*

Bhagavad Gita
3rd teaching

A lot has been said about how to hold your knife in a fight,
and it seems to me this aspect of knife fighting is subject
to the same limited approach that seems to be prevalent
throughout the martial arts. Everybody rants and raves about
why their way is the best way to do it and why any other
way is shit. They won't tell you what its weaknesses and
limitations are. My response has remained consistent
through the years; lift a beer, give 'em a big smile, and say,
"Whatever works."

How you prefer to hold a knife, the weight you like, and
the way the blade is balanced is all your personal choice and
should be based on the way your hand is made. Now, I have
little hands. In fact, they're almost little paws. My fingers
are considerably shorter than my palms, but they are as long
as my palm is wide. Because of that, big-handled knives are
not my first choice. You may have long hands and fingers,
which means a long handle feels just right to you. If you
picked up my knife, you'd wrap your fingers around the handle and that would be it—you'd have no place to put your

palm. Your little finger would be wagging in the wind as well. The point is, you have a particular hand type and size, as well as your own personal preference, which means some things work for you and others don't.

Okay, there are pretty much three basic knife fighting grips that people use. They have pretty standard names, so I can't fuck around with them too much. Mind you, there are other ways to hold a knife, but they are more for ambushes and concealed attacks. Remember, the knife-to-knife fight isn't as common as people think it is. Most of these concealed-attack grips are used to suddenly hurt the guy from left field, then shift to a more conventional grip to finish the job.

Natural Grip

The first type of grip is called the "natural" grip. It is, in essence, just making a fist around the knife. It's not as flexible as the sabre grip, but it makes up for that in another department. The natural grip is less for a slashing and more for a punching style of knife fighting.

Somewhere I remember hearing about a Roman general advising his troops not to bother with a sword's edge other than to wound since it's the point that kills. This assessment was proven correct when they began to dig up graves and discovered that most ancient soldiers had multiple healed slash wounds on their bodies. In most cases, it was thrusts that did them in.

The natural grip is the thrusting grip. When you close with your opponent, you should shift into this grip if you're not already there. This grip particularly comes in handy during a fight when your opponent is wearing a jacket or some other form of "light armor" that renders slashes to the arms and body close to useless. This is the time to poke at legs, the face, and openings in the jacket.

One thing about this grip that I like is that you can "punch" with it. Try it. Get a knife and hold it this way, then throw a punch. Unlike a stab, which is like a tube of danger, a punch thrown with a knife held horizontally becomes an entire *level* that is dangerous. It's not circling out then going back in

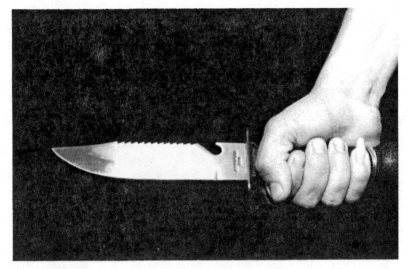

Natural grip.

like a slash, it's slicing straight at the guy. A hook with a knife thrown to the side of a guy's face is going to mess him up pretty bad if done right. If he tries to shed the punch, the blade will shed his nose off.

Another good thing about this grip is that it takes impact well. If you counter into the guy's arm and leather jacket, you're not as likely to get the knife torn out of your hand as you are using the sabre grip. Also (and don't laugh, I've seen the scars where it's happened), you're much less likely to lose your grip and have your fingers slide down onto the blade when you hit something.

The bad thing about the natural grip is that it's not as flexible as the sabre grip. You can't change your edge direction as quickly. That means if you see an opening, you have to change your whole arm's angle to get to it. By that time the opening will probably be gone. It is also much less effective for slashing.

Sabre Grip
Yep, the fencing sword. Same name, same grip. The sabre grip is undoubtedly the most flexible. It's lightning quick for

slashing and direction changes. If you see an opening, you twist your fingers and you're striking and you're there. This grip is tits when it comes to slashes because of the mobility it affords.

Sabre grip.

Another nice thing about the sabre grip is with a flick of the wrist your blade is facing another way. If you strike and the guy dodges, you can flick your wrist and point rip him. Or by the same token, if the guy tries to block your strike or grab your arm, you can whittle him pretty good.

The bad part about this technique is that the blade is somewhat loose in your hands. That means it is more prone to either slip or be knocked from your hand. If you are going to use this grip, you should guard against that as much as possible by choosing a complementary stance. Another disadvantage (at least the way I feel) is that it's not as effective as the natural grip for a solid stab, especially if you don't have a finger guard.

Ice Pick Grip
Gosh, isn't this exciting? All these creative terms! What imaginations these guys must have had!

Now, this is a much maligned grip, but it can be good if it's done edge *out* rather than edge *in*. A major reason this grip got such a bad rap is that when you see someone attacked by a knife murderer in a movie he's carrying the knife this way, but with the edge in. Remember the "psycho in the shower" camera angles? Point down, edge in.

Ice pick grip with the edge in. This limits the grip's effectiveness.

As we know, there's a lot of people out there who don't really think too much on their own. They muddle along through life until they get into a fight. Well, they've seen the movies and they know how it's done. So when they snatch up a knife, what do they do? Right; grab it in the most useless and dangerous way possible—point down, edge in. If they wanted to slash their wrists, they're halfway there. The worst thing about this variation is that if your opponent grabs your wrist, he doesn't even have to turn it; he can just shove and you've stabbed yourself. That much Hollywood did get right. What a surprise, miracles do happen.

Technically, the ice pick grip is not as flexible as the sabre or natural grip. It does have serious striking strength, although it's limited in its possible levels. Another thing is that it is a good cutting technique when combined with a punch, which is pretty much what it's designed for.

Anyway, you have to watch your ass with this grip. If someone comes after you with a knife using this type of grip, you might not see the knife until after you've been cut. Styles that utilize this grip were designed for fighting warriors with swords. In this regard they're really effective.

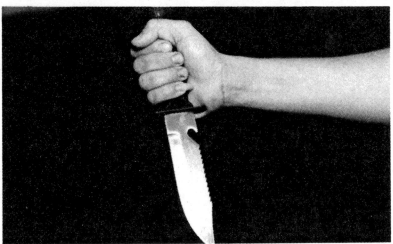

A correct ice pick grip, with the edge pointed out. The knife can be used to stab, slash, and even punch when held in this manner. It is very dangerous.

The Orientals use this grip extensively in their fighting forms, and they prefer to keep the edge out. Now here's something you should know. A thunderin' herd of paramilitary types will tell you that oriental knife fighting techniques ain't shit. While I admit that the military's knife fighting form has some serious advantages in a toe-to-toe cut out, the oriental styles have some serious strong points of their own, especially in the field of ambush.

One more thing that those military types don't like to mention is that the Asian theater is where more Americans have died than any other war theater on this planet. The fact that every time we fight those fuckers, we basically have to resort to bombing the shit out of countries smaller than Illinois should indicate that they are some seriously mean cocksuckers. Don't blow their styles off 'cause some military yutz told you they ain't as good as America. People who use these styles will give you a serious dick chewing if you underestimate them.

Assassin Grips

These grips are the favorite of hit men, convicts, barroom brawlers, shit kickers, bikers, streetfighters, and other charming people.

Assassin grips really aren't fighting grips at all. They're grips that people use to get close without alerting you to the fact that they have a knife. This way they can cut you up a bit to keep you from running or fighting back. Then they can either slice you in a bleed spot and boogie off while you bleed to death, or shift grip and finish you off. So they are mostly for surprise and first strikes. If the strike doesn't work, the user will *probably* shift to something else.

The good thing about defending against assassin grips is that if you get an inkling as to what's going on, they're safer to grab than normal grips. This is why when someone of questionable intent approaches, you should always scan their entire body, especially their hands. Looking at the eyes will give you an idea as to what the guy's up to, but scanning his hands can tell you how he's going to try it. I mean face it, you know the fucker is going to attack you, you don't have to watch the end of the movie. Switch channels to see what else is going on.

A real good way to tell when something is wrong is, if a person is hiding something, *most* times his hand will be stiff in an odd way. Spend a day or two watching the way people's hands move when they're walking. It's kind of a stringy, bouncy motion that's always changing. Then have a friend walk while carrying something concealed—the hand doesn't move.

The following are some of the more popular assassin grips you'll see out there.

Palm Job

No, this is not something you pay a hooker twenty dollars for. If you did you'd change your name to "pencil dick." When someone comes at you with a knife this way, it's to slash you with a slaplike motion. Folding knives are really good for this because they can be manipulated to conform to your hand. This grip is often used to slash at the face and throat (great shock value), though other areas are also open to attack.

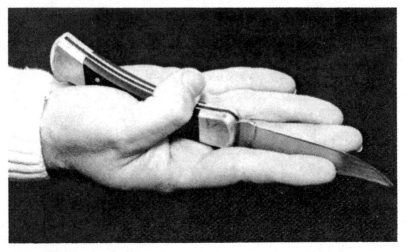

Palm job.

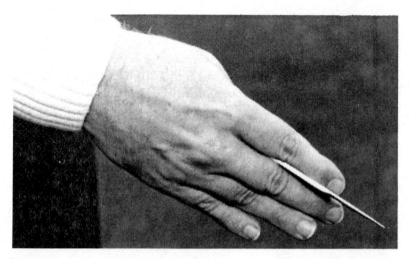

Back view of a palm job.

Palm job at a distance.

The palm job takes some practice to perfect as well as some seriously strong hand muscles. If you're going to practice it, swing at a two-by-four. This will accustom you to the impact of your hand hitting something and show you which muscles you need to exercise. By the way, if you cut the shit out of yourself while practicing, don't blame me. It's one of the weaknesses of this grip.

Peek-a-boo!

I told you I'd screw around with the names. Anyway, this grip is really good for a sudden conversion since it can be used for either slashing or stabbing. My major complaint with it is that you have to do some tricky finger work to shift to another grip. I have seen guys throw the knife forward and catch the handle when they shift grips, but in practice, not in a fight. In an actual fight, I don't like to let go of my blade. I'll shift grips outside of my opponent's strike range, but that's done with finger work, not by throwing my blade around. But remember, I have small hands. It may not work as easily for you.

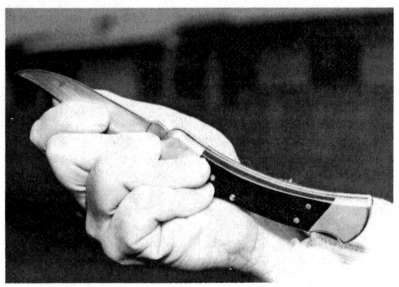

Peek-a-boo grip.

The peek-a-boo grip is how the blade will show up when somebody does a quick draw with their Buck knife. You will encounter it with some frequency, so heads up. The weakness of the peek-a-boo grip is that the hand can be grabbed with relative safety.

Peek-a-boo grip at a distance.

Balisong Boogie

He's little, he's yellow/brown, smells vaguely of fish, has funny shaped eyes, and he's coming after your ass! In his hand is a charming little toy called a *balisong* that he is going to use to decorate the street with pretty red streamers called your guts. The bitch about this is when he gets close enough to make his move, he's going to open his knife into a full-on fighting grip. This is why these blades have become popular with certain unpleasant members of society.

The balisong grip is pretty much the same for switchblades, wheel locks, and stilettos. If anybody approaches you with a closed fist, look the fuck out! Some people may say that I'm overreacting, but if you're in a crowd and somebody comes gunning for you, my advice is to yell, "Look out, knife!" then draw your own. What this does is alert future witnesses to the fact that you're being attacked with a lethal weapon. That way, in court they can say you were defending yourself. Another thing your shout might do is take away the guy's surprise. Most people don't want to get into a toe-to-toe—there's a good chance they'll get cut. Suddenly realizing that it's going to be knife combat instead of an assassination might take the wind out of their sails. If you don't have a knife on you, a beer bottle heaved into the guy's chest as you're pointing out the fact that he has a knife is almost as good a deterrent.

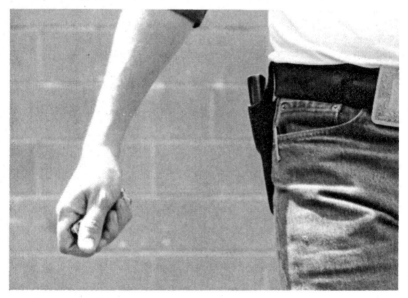

Balisong boogie.

The one real weakness of the balisong grip is if someone knows what to look for, they'll know to attack before the weapon is brought into play. A strike to the hand is really effective in preventing the completion of the move. By the way, if *you're* doing the move, it should be done at waist level. It's harder for somebody to take your knife away while it's being opened at that level. Don't laugh, I've seen it happen.

Balisong boogie at a distance.

Hide-a-blade

Yep, the old ice pick grip is back to haunt you. This is where it works the best. With this grip, you don't see the knife until you're either cut or about to be. The reverse slash you already know about, but the reason I mention the ice pick grip in this context is because it's a good way to conceal a fixed-bladed knife. You can also spin the knife in your hand to shift grip. This spin calls for practice, but you can practice when you're watching TV, so there are lots of people who can do it real well.

You will notice I said spin, not flip. Flipping a blade is when you toss it in the air and catch it to change its direction, something you should never do. A spin, however, is done entirely in the hand by finger motion. At no time does the knife leave your hand. You are less likely to drop it if you're struck while doing the shift.

Except that it's done with a fixed blade, the hide-a-blade grip is basically the same thing as the balisong boogie.

Hide-a-blade (also leopard grip) at a distance.

Wino Waltz

This is a real cocksucker because of its very appearance. It looks like the guy is wandering around with a bottle of booze when in actuality he has an ice pick or stilleto with your name on it. The blade is driven in and the person just walks away. Nobody notices shit until you either scream or collapse. By that time the knifer is long gone. Someone staggering up to you looking drunk should always be watched, especially if you're not somebody's favorite candidate for the living.

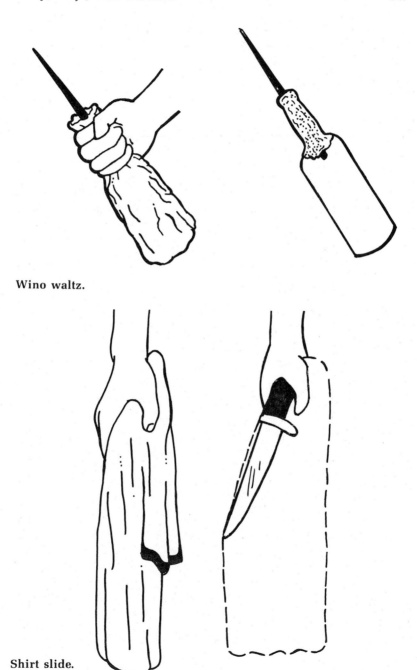

Wino waltz.

Shirt slide.

Shirt Slide

This is another that you have to watch for, especially at beaches or other places where it's common to see somebody wandering around with their shirt off. The knife is hidden in the folds of the shirt. When the blow is struck, the blade cuts through the shirt and into you. Not good. Again, this is one of those moves that because it looks so normal nobody will notice the guy who did it, especially if he's smart and walks away instead of running.

Leopard Grip

This is sort of like a blend between the oriental version of the ice pick and the Balisong Boogie. I personally don't like it because it leaves the hand wide open for a counterstrike. To transfer into a natural or sabre grip you have to let the blade fall forward and catch it. To take it to the oriental grip, all you have to do is let it drop into your palm. It's closer to a natural hand position than most of the other assassin grips, so it's a little harder to spot.

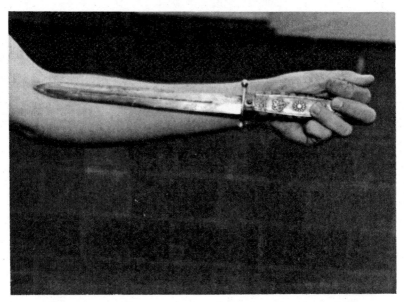

Leopard grip.

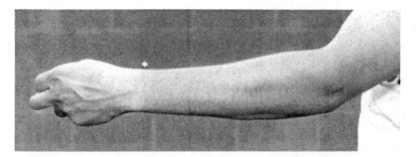

Back view of a leopard grip.

Punch Grips

There are a lot of variations of these kinds of grips. For the most part they are for first-move assassin punches. There you are and suddenly, "Surprise!" They can be used for slashes, but it's sort of a twitchy proposition. The fingers are supposed to act as a grip but often act as a pivot point instead. The knife can either twist and cut you or spin out of your hand if your thumb isn't strong enough. If someone can catch your hand while you're using one of these grips, all I have to say is I hope you made out your will, because odds are it's going to be a slow march and loud singing for you.

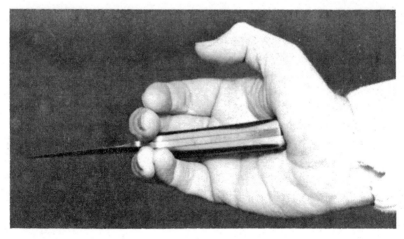

Punch grip (open).

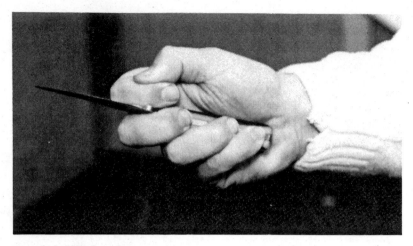

Punch grip (closed).

* * * * *

Weight and balance are really a matter of personal taste. Some people prefer the weight and balance in the point, others in the handle, while still others prefer it in the middle. Some like heavy knives while others like light slicers. It's up to you. I personally ride with a small, heavy blade with the weight and balance in the front part of the handle. It works for me. What works for you is probably going to be different.

Finding the point of balance is easy. Hold a knife across your finger and try to balance it. When it stays, you've found that blade's point of balance. Don't do it with just your own knife. Go out and do it with every knife you pick up. This is important. It trains you to instinctively check for the balance of a blade while in your hand. Working this way you will begin to sense what you will have to do with a knife to make it work for you. In time, your hand will begin to gravitate to the point where your hand feels most comfortable on the knife, and soon you will be doing it by instinct.

Another way to train your body is to intentionally grab knives incorrectly. From there you adjust to the correct grip. This teaches your body to feel that something is wrong as well as how to make corrections. This instinctive knowledge,

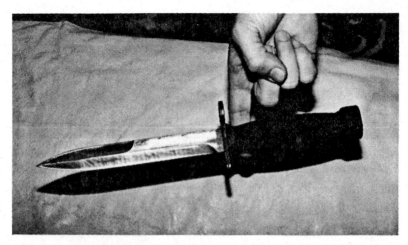

A knife's point of balance is really a matter of personal taste. Many people prefer the point shown here. I like it further back on the handle.

as you'll find out in the quick draw chapter, is critical to getting your knife out fast. If you don't instinctively know what different "wrongs" feel like and how to adjust to get them "right," you'll freeze for a moment when you encounter them, which could easily get you killed.

I lie to you not; one of the things about body habits is if something goes wrong, the clutch slips until your mind can be turned back on again. If you don't believe me, try this test. Wait until someone you know gets ready to smoke a cigarette. The motions of taking out and lighting a cigarette have become so well-ingrained, the person doesn't have to think about it—he/she just does it quickly and easily.

Now, here's the test. Between the time the cigarette is put in the person's mouth and the time he lights it, take the cigarette out of his mouth and hold it up in front of him. I swear you'll get a busy signal for at least a second. Then the person's brain will kick in and he'll look at you real annoyed like. Explain to him what you were doing and why. That second of freeze frame is what I'm talking about. If you don't train your body to react to the variables that you'll encounter, you'll freeze at a critical moment.

Chapter Seven

▼

Stance

Discipline is a means to an end, not an end unto itself.
King Crimson

Time to get your rubber knives and your buddy again and practice stances. When I say practice something in this book, I don't mean just half an hour one day and then skip to the next stage. Spend about a week doing it until you're really good at it. I also mean in various mental states: tired, angry, worried, and so on. While we're at it, practice these things in whatever chemically altered state you're likely to find yourself. For those of you who think I just said (gasp) drugs, you're right! Drugs also include booze, caffeine, and tobacco; and lack of food, a full stomach, sleep, and sex bring about different kinds of chemically altered states. All of these involve chemical reactions in your body.

The stance you use is really determined by personal prefer-ence and your particular style of knife fighting. I can share with you some insights I have gained into various stances over the years. This includes strong points and weak points, as well as some of the best ways around the strong points of different stances.

I'll be talking about "slipping" a lot. Slipping is when you slide past the guy's knife to one side or the other. Certain stances are really susceptible to getting slipped.

Another thing I'll be talking about is target areas. Certain stances leave certain areas open while covering other areas. This is something you should know about because if you leave a spot open, it'll get cut. Most of the stances I know of consist of crouching down, which protects a number of vital spots by its very position.

Yet another thing that I'll yap about is stance integrity. What this means is the ability of the stance (via the position of the feet) to resist a blow coming in from the direction that you're facing. Good stance integrity will allow you to absorb the energy of a blow (by grounding it) and remain as you were. Bad stance integrity is when someone hits you from the front and you end up shining the sidewalk with your butt.

Hollywood Stance

This is probably the best way I know to get kicked in the nuts and have your knife taken away. It's also a great way to get dissected up the middle. If that's not enough, another disadvantage is that you can get your knife hand and arm cut to shit real quick. Also, since the guard is so high up, it leaves your legs and knees wide open to attack.

Most people are seriously off balance when they start this pose. Because of the position of the feet, it's real easy to grab the guy's arm and jerk him off balance. If your opponent sideslips you to the left, you have to cross yourself to strike back at him (good luck). Speaking of sideslipping, you only have one line in this stance, and it's both your offensive and defensive line. If it's slipped, in a word, you're fucked.

The strong point of this stance is it looks great, just like in the movies.

Close, But No Cigar

This basically is a variation of the Hollywood stance, with a little of the Oriental stance thrown in. Unfortunately, it combines the worst aspects of both. This stance, or

Hollywood stance (front view). As you can see, this stance leaves a direct opening along the body's center line, and the inside of the arms are vulnerable. If an experienced knife fighter hesitates to attack someone using this stance, it isn't because he's scared—he's probably trying to decide what primo target to cut off.

Hollywood stance (top view).

something like it, is common for inexperienced knife fighters to fall into. The same problems of balance and crossing exist here along with the hassle of lack of low guard and related problems. The advantage of this stance over the Hollywood is it gives you two lines. Your left arm acts as a shield to protect you, while your right is left free to attack. Also, your knife arm is less susceptible to attack.

"Close, but no cigar" stance (front view). With this stance, the most open targets are the left arm and anything below the dick. After that, you can move into more primary targets.

"Close, but no cigar" stance (top view).

Oriental Stance

You seldom see a person with slanty eyes in this position. More often you'll see some cockstrong martial artist strike this pose. (This gives you a chance to get a good snapshot. A picture is worth a thousand words, after all.) The oriental stance has only one weakness—the entire left side. Other than that it's balanced, semimobile, flexible, absolutely devastating on the right side, multilined, and looks great.

Many martial artists know this is a starting stance to launch an attack from; defensively speaking, it's weak. The major weakness is that it is easy to grab the left arm and jerk it across the body, thus leaving the entire left side open and vulnerable to a knife thrust. Also, one of the problems it shares with the first two stances is predictability. Most people broadcast when they're about to make a move, usually by a shift in the shoulders. With everything up high and out in the open, it's really easy to spot what the guy is about to throw at you.

This is a good time to remember that the soldiers of the Orient carried swords for thousands of years. About half of the moves are designed to fight a guy with a long sword, not another knife.

Oriental stance (front view). You can tell people who use this stance watch reruns of "Kung Fu" on television. But be wary—stay away from his right side and watch out for kicks. Be careful of slashing at the left arm. It's there to tempt you so he can grab your knife hand when you try it. Instead, you can try to slip to the left and grab his left arm. If you miss, he can break your jaw with his elbow. If you succeed, immediately jerk him off balance (which you should *always* do when you grab someone during a knife fight).

Oriental stance (top view).

One of the main reasons why I dislike the oriental and "close, but no cigar" stances is because they both leave the legs open as targets. By crossing and trapping your opponent's left arm against his body, you can easily hamstring him. If you strike higher on the body, it's more likely to be fatal.

Oriental stance #2 (front view). Targeting on this one is a little tricky because you're going to get cut while getting close to the guy. The left side is your best bet. This stance is meant to lure you in to attack, because one of its main strengths is the ability to counter.

Oriental stance #3 (top view).

Oriental Stance #2

This is one you're more likely to see someone of oriental persuasion in. If you're not careful, it'll be the last thing you see. One of the reasons paramilitary types say that oriental knife fighting styles aren't any good is because they're more Californian—meaning laid back and casual, for those of you who were wondering. An oriental stylist will slice you up a bit before he gets around to killing you. "It's no rush. I mean, hey, maybe you don't want to die, so I'll give you a chance to leave with only a little blood loss." The military attitude, on the other hand, is more New York, which means, "I want him dead *now*, Goddamn it!" (It must be all that cocaine coming in from Florida that makes New Yorkers impatient.)

One nice thing about this stance is it's really aggressive defensively, sort of like sticking your arm down a badger hole. That's because it's really good for counters. Due to the positioning of the hands (and knife), it gives good cover. I'm not so hot on it offensive wise because it really does wait for the other guy to make the first move.

If you get close to someone using this style you are going to get cut, which is why if you see somebody drop into this or some related stance, you had better decide if it's worth it. The only real safe way to deal with this is to get the fuck out of there. The less-than-safe way is to accept that you're going to get cut and go into combat mode. If you try to dick around with being macho man, you're going to get your dick sliced off.

The real bitch about this stance is that the knife is not visible. If the guy is good, you'll never know that he's got a knife until it's too late. You'll never see it slip into his hand unless you were watching real close. So be alert and careful.

Military Stance

Those of you in the military will probably recognize this one. All joking aside as to how the military usually does things ("Honey, have you seen the D9 Cat? I have to move something."), they did this one right. This is my personal choice for stance. It's quick, sneaky, good defensively, and you can really be an offensive fucker with it.

The left arm is out there as a shield, buffer zone, and grabber—you can use it to block or seize your opponent's attacks. It is also a physical barrier against rushes. The guy rushing you encounters resistance and is slowed down. In the meantime, you're puncturing him repeatedly. The left arm is also a trap. It looks real tempting as a target, but if someone goes for it he'll get sliced for his trouble. The way the arm is held and turned to parry presents little that is actually damaging. A knife hitting this area will cut skin only, then bounce off the bone. Major muscles, tendons, and arteries are behind the guard. If someone manages to score, they will only cut muscles that relate to the little and ring fingers, leaving your two strongest fingers and thumb intact.

The military stance is mobile and balanced. It also either protects or moves out of effective range many of your most vulnerable target areas. It's harder to slip effectively because

Military stance (front view). Looks tempting, doesn't it? Don't try it, though. That arm is a lure for your knife arm. When you close with somebody in this stance, he will slip into the short timer and be ready to rock and roll.

Military stance (top view).

of where the blade is held (an upper rip is a pretty good deterrent). It also protects your knife arm from attack.

Offensively speaking, the military stance is deceptive. The knife can end up anywhere from its starting position. Levels change by straightening or bending the legs while striking. You can close by stepping in, and as you do your knife travels with you. If the stance has any generic weaknesses, I sure 'n hell haven't found 'em. By generic weakness I don't mean mistakes that the individual using the style makes. I'm talking aspects that can be consistently exploited to take someone out who is using the style. If you know of any, write me and tell me about them. I'd love to know.

Short Timer

This is a slight variation of the military stance that I have seen. The reason I call it "short timer" is because it is often preferred by shorter people. It isn't as effective overall as the military stance because it is shallower in defense. People with

Short timer stance (front view). Other than the fact that the knife arm is more exposed, this is pretty much the same as the military stance.

Short timer stance (top view).

shorter arms often make this change to allow them to strike faster. This speed is counterbalanced by increased exposure of vital spots. Also, because the right leg leads, the knife is closer to the front, which makes it more susceptible to attack. It's also easier to get off balance in this stance due to a tendency to lean too far forward. If you can compensate for these differences, however, it works very well.

Pissed-off Stance

This actually isn't a stance per say, but if you don't know it you'll be crying "Medic!" real quick. It's mostly for a first strike rather than a knife fight. You can't see the knife until the person strikes, and if it's a blackened blade you might not know he had one till after you're cut.

I know of a guy who was sitting in a bar when some tough guy came in gunning for trouble. Tough guy spotted the person, who happened to be the smallest guy in the bar (it's either that or something happened earlier that wasn't men-

Pissed-off stance (front view).

Pissed-off stance (side view).

tioned). Tough guy walks up and just hauls off and hits the shorter guy. Short guy staggers back and in the process crosses his arms. He stops and looks at tough guy. Tough guy comes at him again. Short guy punches tough guy in the chest. Tough guy falls down. Short guy walks out of the bar. A few minutes later tough guy is still on the floor and short guy walks back in. They roll tough guy over and discover he has a new name: dead guy. The police are called and they know who did it, but nobody ever saw a weapon and no weapon is ever found. Short guy says he didn't do it. Can't prove anything, so short guys walks. Dead guy is buried for his stupidity. End of story.

Crossing the arms is a natural action when someone is pissed off. As the story illustrates, however, it can also put you in the high risk zone. If someone begins to cross their arms, stop them by calling them on it or just haul off and hit the motherfucker hard and with everything you got. Better to be arrested for fighting than dead by stabbing. Remember the story I told you about at the beginning of this book? I know from experience on this one.

Subway Pass

This also is not a fighting stance but rather a serious first-move threat. The subway pass is a way to take someone out who isn't paying attention to you. If you've jammed with someone who is a gang member or something exciting like that, you could be at risk because one of his buddies who you don't recognize may come after you.

The blade is held in an oriental grip, and the hands are in the pockets. (My aren't we casual.) As the person approaches you, they begin to spin. The blade sinks into you and the spin continues on. The person who just stabbed you walks away and nobody has seen his or her face. If something goes wrong with this maneuver, however, the person doing it is in a position known in strategic terminology as "fucked." They can't move away fast enough to keep from getting eviscerated themselves or kicked in the crotch so hard that their nuts end up in their cheeks.

In a subway pass, the subject approaches with his hands in his pockets.

He starts to spin. The knife is being removed from his pocket, though it is still concealed from the victim's view.

At the completion of the spin, the knife is out and the subject stabs the victim.

Chapter Eight

▼

Quickdraw

Aye Evrybody, ees Quickdraw!
    "Doc" teasing a wannabe cowboy who
    had shot himself in the foot while
    practicing quickdraw.

Most people think that having a weapon is the same thing as being able to get to it. WRONG! *A weapon that you can't get out in time is the same as no weapon at all.* One of the most common mistakes people make is that they practice fighting up one side and down the other but totally ignore draw! The same is twenty times as true with people and guns.

Let's look at something here. If you jam with somebody and they've got MPS, you could be in for some shit. If they know that you're dangerous and usually armed, they're going to come after you out of the shadows with no warning. The truth is, *the "badder" you are the more likely somebody's going to try to take you out suddenly and from behind.*

In my old neighborhood there was a guy who was one of the most vicious sons of a bitch that at the time I had ever seen. This guy was pure hell on wheels. Anybody who went head-to-head with this guy got seriously hurt. Well, he was so bad that one night somebody snuck up behind him in the alley behind his house and blew his brains out. What the tough guy had overlooked was that being bad isn't enough—

you also have to be aware. This guy was so sure that nobody would mess with him that he got sloppy and left his back door open. His family had to clean what was left of him off the wall because of his stupidity. If you're dangerous, the way to stay that way is to stay alive. The way to do that is to assume that somebody is most likely going to take a crack at you from one of your blind spots.

One of the best ways to save your ass from a sudden attack is to work on quickly getting your weapon out and into play. (The other aspect is awareness, which I've gone over in my first book.) The basics are applicable to both folded and fixed blades so I'm not going to make much of a differentiation.

Step one about quickdraw is *instinctively knowing where your knife is at all times.* This is more specific than "Oh, on my belt on my right side." This is the body instincts we spoke about earlier but now applied to draw. The best way to get familiar with your knife is to repeatedly draw it and put it back until you begin to sense where it is.

There are some things you can do to make this training easier. One: as tempting as it is to see what an awesome badass you are, *don't practice in front of the mirror.* The reason you should practice without a mirror is actually quite valid. It trains your body to operate without visual aid, so you have to rely on your body's awareness of the weight and drag that the knife and sheath create. It will hone your instinctive feel for your weapon.

The next point is: *don't look at your sheath when you resheath your knife.* This is the same learning process as the draw, except in reverse. Odd as it may seem, your body doesn't care which way it learns something. By not looking at your sheath you can cut your learning time in half. Then you can go practice your truculent sneers in the mirror. (I hadn't done the mirror bit in a long time when one day while unloading a van in Hollywood, I caught a flicker of something out of the corner of my eye. It was somebody who had every move, marking, and attitude of a vicious mother-fucker and he was nearly in my blindspot. I dropped what I had in my arms and spun, ready to fight off a serious attack, only to realize that I had nearly knifed a mirrored store window and managed to scare the shit out of myself in the process. I still use mirrors; I just feel more stupid about it than you should.)

Another thing about quickdraw you want to consider is that the fastest draws are the ones that have the least excess motion. This is true for life in general but can be applied to knife fighting. The fastest techniques are the simplest techniques. You don't become fast by going faster—you become fast by figuring out ways to streamline the motion to a bare minimum. I don't care how fast you are, if you have to do three things to get your knife out and I only have to do one, I'm going to win on the draw. You have three things that can go wrong while I only have one.

One way to cut excess motion is to move in circles rather than lines. It may sound weird but a tight loop is faster than a start, stop, restart, stop. Actually when you see it in black and white, it doesn't look all that unbelievable, does it?

By removing possible burrs from the system, you won't get hung up by one of them jamming the works. This is the same argument between automatic pistols and revolvers, one side voting for fast reloads and more firepower, the other for no jamming and an almost guaranteed first shot. So when you practice your draw, begin to look for action that you can lose from the process.

A very good example is to look at the way most people carry their Buck knives. In the normal position, you have to sweep your hand up, catch the flap with your index finger, and push it out of the way. Then your thumb and index finger have to pinch the back edge of the blade hard enough to pull it up and out. Once there, you have to snap your wrist to open the knife. Now, where in that process can something go wrong if you're in a hurry?

Let's look at the other kind of draw for a Buck knife. Ever notice the wolves who walk among men? I mean, officially they're human beings, but something about them spells wild animal. If you look at their belts you'll begin to notice the number of them who carry their sheaths upside down. This

is an important safety tip: these guys are dangerous. All one
has to do is drop a hand down and with the little finger brush
open the sheath flap, then catch the falling knife by the blade
and snap it open. Guess which one is faster and has less
jams in the system?

Undoubtedly, the fastest way to do something is to break
it down into base components and blend them into a single
move. This is mostly for belt knives, but take the basics here
and apply them to however you carry your rig. (By the way,
you should be intimately familiar with your knife's balance
and know the difference between right and wrong grips
before moving to this part of your training.)

When you draw a sheath knife, sweep your hand up from
below and behind. When your palm and little finger hit the
knife handle, begin to close your little and ring fingers against
the knife. This pushes the blade into the palm of your hand.
Now, without stopping, start drawing the knife out of the
sheath. Keep moving forward with the action, all the while
keeping a loose wrist. The tip of the knife should brush
against the top of the sheath. It'll sometimes give a little jerk
as it leaves. If your wrist isn't loose enough to act as a shock
absorber for this jerk, the knife might just springboard out
of your hand into your foot. Now that you're clear of the
sheath, wrap your fingers around the handle and slide into
your preferred grip.

The draw I have just described is accomplished in one motion. In emergency situations I have been able to get my knife
in my hand and into fighting position in slightly less than
a second. There have been times when my knife got into my
hand so fast that I didn't even remember drawing it. That
is why I'm such a son of a bitch in an ambush. My body
acts before I know what the fuck is going on; I'm just along
for the ride. My body is taking care of everything while my
mind is going, "Hey, what's going on?"

You should practice your draw anytime you have a chance.
If you're doing laundry in the Laundromat, practice drawing and resheathing. If you're at work try it there. Don't make
a production of it, just do it quietly. If you're waiting for the

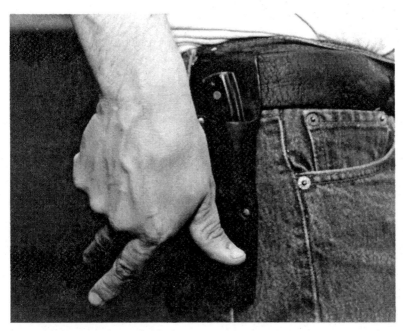

Starting point for a quickdraw.

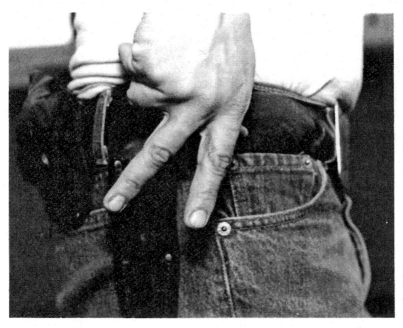

Grabbing the knife.

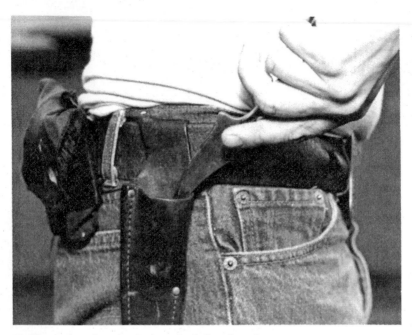

Knife tip brushes against top of the sheath.

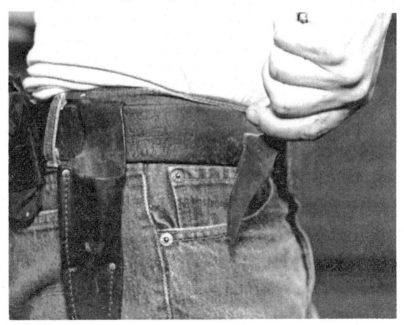

Fingers wrap around the handle.

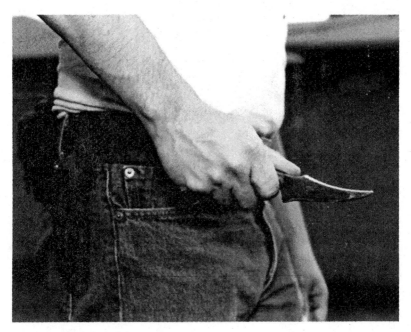

A completed quickdraw.

old lady at the store, step behind some clothes racks and go kersnickity-snack for a bit. Just get used to doing it anywhere. Also, when you have to draw your knife to do something (as opposed to doing somebody), use your fighting draw until you just plain old draw that way always. From there it's only a matter of speeding up the process in an emergency.

A standard you should set for yourself is to get your draws down to about two seconds from start to application. First trim off the fat, then start working on speed. Do this from all the positions in which you regularly find yourself. It'll teach you what you need to do in order to improve and train your body to react from any position. This is so if somebody tries to surprise you, your body will know all the variables it might encounter in any given position and how to compensate for them. For example, my knife handle moves up to one inch from it's normal position when I'm sitting down, which changes the draw angle considerably. How do you think that would affect your quickdraw?

Once you've spent a month or so knocking your draw down

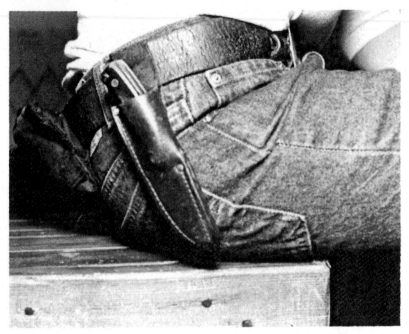

Just by sitting down, you've shifted the position of the knife handle. You must experience these small shifts in order for you to know where your knife is at all times. Practice drawing and resheathing your knife from a sitting position and you'll see what I mean.

to a reasonable speed, it's time for the next step. Again, don't skip forward too fast on this training. Don't move on to the next step until you have the immediate one down pat. If you don't have a solid foundation, it's going to crumble at the worst possible time, like when you're in the shit. I swear to God, most people I know who got nailed did so because they disregarded the basics. We're not talking about if you make a mistake the teacher gives you an "F," we're talking if you blow it you get a little tag hanging off your toe.

Chapter Nine

▼

Draws

Einstein's Theory of Reality: R = Shit Happens.
The best variation I've seen so far.

A lot of people talk about all the neat ways to draw your knife. For some reason they leave out what a streetfighter will do to you when he sees you going for a knife that way. This makes me wonder about some of these people's qualifications to teach fighting and/or self-defense. "Like, how many times you actually done this, Bub?" There are a lot of things that can go wrong and unless you know about them beforehand, you can get killed. I am curious: are these people that inexperienced in street knife fighting or are they leaving it out on purpose? Evidently there's an attitude about not telling people the truth because it'll scare them. Well in the same sense I feel that people should be jailed for telling lies to children, I feel people should be shot for not telling the truth about fighting, especially knife fighting.

In reality, there's a heap'a shit that can go wrong during a knife fight. If you go for your knife and I don't have one, I'm not going to grab a short club and try to grapple with you. I'm going to hop back three steps, pick up a half-filled beer bottle, and peg it right between your eyes real fuckin' hard. That'll put a dent in your quickdraw as well as your hat. Certain types of draws are really susceptible to a rush. If I can get my hands on you before you can get your knife out, you're going to be in a world of hurt. Another thing is you can get slammed up against a wall and not be able to get to your knife. (I know all of them from experience. The first two I showed other people why it wasn't a smart idea to try and pull a knife on me, the third I had demonstrated to me. Ouch.)

The point is that you need to learn how to contend with variables. Make a sheath for your rubber knife and use it in the same manner you carry your real knife. Then have your ever-present training buddy try and fuck up your attempts to draw. Do this all over the place—in the kitchen, front yard, hallway, living room, car (preferably while it's parked), Laundromat, and so on. Mess around with it until you get the idea of what it takes to jam a draw. This will let you know what you have to do in certain situations to prevent countermeasures from getting sprung on you. After a while you get wary of anybody getting into a position where they could block you.

Cross Draw

I don't like this draw for a number of reasons. The first one is that it sets up a flare as to what you're about to do. Because of this, your opponent's got enough time to finish his beer before he bodychecks you. Or he might just decide to pick up a bar stool and brain you with it. (These sorts are really rude. They don't even have the manners to thank you for letting them know your intentions so far in advance.) The cross draw is also really susceptible to a rush that pins your right arm against your body.

The other thing I dislike about the cross draw is it's hard to do in one motion. You could play super samurai and try, but it's a little cranky to perfect. This makes it slower than most draws. The reason it works with swords is that they're longer than knives so you need more room to get one out of its scabbard.

Cross draw.

Another thing I have found irritating about this draw is that you need to put the knife all the way across the left side of your body or it gets in the fuckin' way, especially when you sit. Seriously, it jabs you in the thigh when you sit down unless you have it rigged right. Maybe you can figure out some way to make this work. Just know what you're up against.

The good point of this draw is that it's perfect for doing a deep slash at stomach level.

Boot Knife

Unless you wear your weapon strapped outside your boot and your pants tucked in, do yourself a favor and don't bother to carry a knife this way. A boot knife is best when used as a backup weapon. Yes, I mean carrying two or more knives. The boot knife is easily accessible only if you're sitting down. That way you can quietly draw it without much fuss so when you stand up you have an ugly surprise for the fucker.

There are a variety of reasons why I'm saying these negative things, mostly from personal experience. I once had to get to a knife I had strapped at my boot. I thought I was being slick by rigging it so it hung upside down. I had seen guys try to pull up their pant legs and get to their knives before. I'd also seen them get taken out real fast. So I rigged it so I didn't have to pull up my pant leg to get to my knife. Wasn't I a smart little whip-dick?

Well shit happened, as it's prone to do in Venice, California, and I went for my knife. I had it rigged upside down on the inside of my left leg. (It shows too much on the right outside. Police notice strange lumps like that.) Anyway, I went for my knife by lifting my leg up and grabbing for it. I lost my balance. Imagine if you will a young cockstrong street punk bunny hopping backward on one leg through some stranger's kitchen during a party while clawing at his ankle. Yes, that is what happened. Fortunately others broke up the fight before I could get my weapon out or he died laughing.

Another incident also happened at a party when two kids got into a jam. One kid went for a knife at his boot. My partner and I were bouncing the party and we looked at each other for a moment in disbelief. *People still do that?* My friend walked up and shoved the guy down onto the ground. I walked up to the other guy and shook my head to say, "Fighting is a Bozo no-no."

I've also seen people blown off their feet by a front snap kick to their face for bending over during a fight. I tell you seriously; this is a backup position for your knife. Capisce?

Belt

Here it is, the bread and butter, the most common of all knife positions. There are a lot of people who don't like to carry their knives on their belt, though. They feel it takes too long to draw it up and out, then drop down into position. There is something to be said about this attitude. Under certain conditions it is true, so you should know about them.

Most of the people who don't like the belt position aren't carrying knives, they're carrying short swords. Trying to get a pig sticker out of a sheath is somewhat of a slow and complicated process. (It's also sort of gawky, which makes it hard to look cool while whipping out something big enough to scare Crocodile Dundee.) That is one very real problem.

Another problem is until sheaths are broken in, they make it sort of necessary to draw your knife up then out, which is slower. The third reason some people don't like the belt position has to do with their build. I've noticed a number of them are either short waisted, or their arms are longer than normal in proportion to their body. There are still other reasons, mostly having to do with the psychological impact on the other guy.

There are always options to consider. One is get a smaller knife. If you have a job as a professional buffalo skinner I can understand carrying a Bowie or survival knife, but in the city? The other is to work your sheath until it moves with your body easily. This gets rid of the stiffness and makes it easier to move. After all, it's the sheath that lies at the core of most of the complaints.

The third option not only works for people with physical

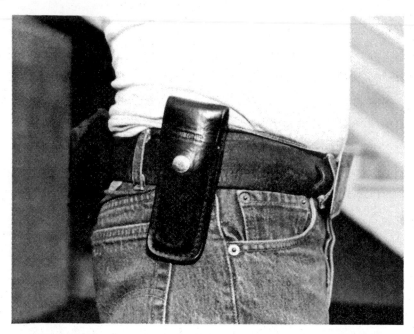

A folding knife carried on the belt.

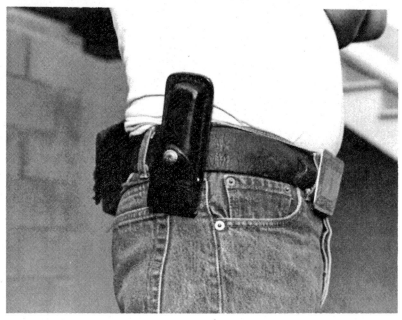

A folding knife carried upside down for a speed draw.

differences but also solves the sheath problem. Face it, there are some great knives put into crappy sheaths. If you're uncomfortable with the way your knife feels on the draw, check it out. Is it too high up? Does the loop make it ride further up than what you are comfortable with? If so, get a new sheath for it. There are leather makers who will rig up any type of harness that you can dream up to.make it more comfortable for you. The way I check to find where somebody wants to have their knife ride is to have them put on another belt (with the knife attached) lower or higher than where they usually wear their belt. Fish around till you find what feels right and then make a sheath to match those specs.

One of the things I like about the side draw from the belt is that you can turn your knife side away and get your blade out without too much hassle. Along those same lines, there is something I should warn you about. If you travel a lot between different social levels, you will encounter something that is *really fucking stupid*. People (in the middle class especially) have no concept of weapon etiquette. By that I mean you don't touch someone's weapon without asking. I have had more people walk up and try to pull my knife than you (or even I for that matter) would believe. It flabbergasted me the first time somebody walked up to me and as a *joke* tried to pull my knife! I swear I almost crushed the guy's thorax. I was able to stop in time when I 1) recognized him, and 2) realized he wasn't reacting to being attacked. (He was middle class. He didn't realize what was about to happen to him so he didn't even flinch.) He thought it would be funny to say "Hi" to me that way.

Another time I slammed a woman I worked with against a wall. I was working on something in a walkway when she passed behind me and playfully gave my knife a tug. I had her up against the wall with my arm across her throat before either of us knew what was happening.

The advantage to the side position is that you can slap people's hands away if they try this stupid shit. Another thing I like about it is that you can shove your rig up against a belt loop and have a solid idea of where it is at all times.

During the day brush against it and push it back into place. Again, this trains your body to always know where your weapon is.

Back Draw

I used to carry my knife like this for years. In time I gradually shifted to the side because of stupid people grabbing for my knife. This was more to protect others from my reactions than to protect against actual attack. This is a great position for a quick draw, especially with a custom sheath at an upward angle. Also, when you first meet people who normally don't carry knives, you can impress them with your wit, charm, and personality before they see that you are carrying a knife. The only real disadvantage about this position is that it does leave your knife open for a grab, and not all the people grabbing for it will be friendly.

Back draw.

Harness

This is one of those personal calls again. If you wear a rig that you can carry on your left breast, it makes for a mothering fast draw. Also, it's just a drop away from the military stance. This and other reasons are why the elite often carry their blades in this position. There is a problem, though. Unless you're doing something the government officially frowns on (but privately supports), people are going to frown on you for carrying a blade like this. After all, this isn't Central America. If you intend to go on a paid mission soon, maybe you should practice it. If you're just going to the corner store, you're going to scare the taxpayers if you carry it this way.

The second variation is the shoulder harness. The first rule of carrying your weapon this way is simple: *don't close your jacket!* If you carry your knife this way with your jacket closed

Harnass draw (military version).

and need to get it out quick, you're screwed, if not for the fact that it takes too much time, then for the fact that the guy will know you're going for something and land on you harder 'n shit. Another thing that worries me about this is somebody might decide you're going for a gun and go for theirs first. Bringing a knife to a gun fight is a bad idea. A shoulder harness is also susceptible to rushes in the same manner that a cross draw is. If you need to draw a knife this way, skip back a few steps to foil any attempted bodychecks.

These small disadvantages aside, there are two ways to carry a knife in a harness: handle up and handle down.

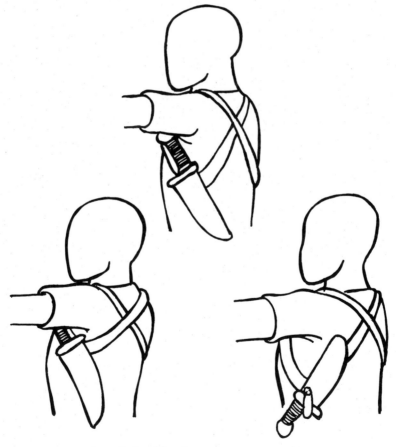

Various examples of shoulder harnesses.

Which one is faster depends on the particulars of the sheath, like if it has a snap tie down. The handle up may or may not need the snap. With the handle down . . . nah, I can't say it. It's too obvious. With the handle down you have gravity speeding up the process of getting the mother out. Handle down is also closer to the military stance, while handle up is great for opening the conversation with a face slash.

One more thing I should tell you about the handle-up rig. I've done this, so I know it happens. Be careful if you draw it in a hurry. Unlike a gun, a knife has an edge. For the fastest form of this draw, the blade is carried edge to the back or, for smaller knives, at an upward angle. When you whip it out you can slice yourself pretty good. I went through a T-shirt and partly into me on that one.

Concealed Weapons

When I discovered that there's a difference between a knife fighter and a punk with a blade, I quit carrying my knives concealed. I also eventually realized that if I needed my knife in a hurry, I couldn't get to it in time when using most forms of concealment.

Concealment is a highly overrated situation. I have tried a wide range of forms and configurations. Some of them worked better than others, but none where I could consistently get to my knife within two seconds in an emergency situation. For years I tried to find a way to rig up a concealed system that I could get to consistently in an emergency and where I wouldn't end up losing my knife somehow. It finally got to the point where I just said "Fuck it, I'll deal with the cops. It's better than being dead."

Well, I've come to realize that there are some places that a knife is not an acceptable addition to an ensemble. From bitter personal experience I've also found that when people tell you not to bring a weapon, bring two. While that is an overstatement, my knife is now as much a part of me as my thumb. This means I use it a lot and I get upset when people try to tell me I can't bring it with me.

I have to admit, most times that you carry a concealed

weapon you really don't need one, but it goes against the grain to leave the house without something. One of the best ways around this impasse is to carry a folding knife in your pocket. Unless you're frisked, nobody is going to know about it. The thing about carrying any kind of concealed weapon is you need to go to Code Yellow. Since you know it will take extra time to get the weapon out and into operation, you have to be especially careful about watching what's going on around you.

Don't let anybody close to you if you go for a concealed knife. It's better to hit the guy a few times and run like fuck while drawing it. If the guy is dumb enough to follow, you can then turn and fight. (Shit, if you can, keep running. You got a three step lead headin' to the door, why not take it? "Gimme three steps mister, gimme three steps toward the door. . .") If you can't run while drawing a concealed weapon, you should backpedal at least three to four feet.

Sometimes you won't have time to go for your weapon. All you can do in this situation is come in with a few bare-handed kill shots and don't even bother with your weapon. Remember, most people are stabbed while trying to get their weapon out instead of defending themselves. If the guy pulls a knife on you he's either expecting you to freak or run away immediately. He's probably not expecting you to crush his windpipe. Because of that fact, most people are real sloppy with their guard against an unarmed opponent.

Basically, I don't advocate carrying a concealed weapon as the norm. For the exception, yes, but not all the time. Here are some of my experiences with different types of concealed carries. Tucked in the waistband: a cold knife sliding down my pant leg or falling out onto the ground. In my sock: sliding down into my shoe, making it 1) uncomfortable, 2) inaccessible, and 3) make me look stupid while taking my shoe off to get my knife out. Under my shirt: the guard snagging up in my shirt during draw. Upside-down rigs in general: lost knives. Sleeve rigs: the blade slipping down my wrist and into view (once, falling onto the table). Buckle knife: fighting to get it out, and having it fall on the floor in front of witnesses while I was taking a piss.

Besides these specific problems, concealed weapons in general will make funny bulges in your clothing that a blind man could spot from thirty feet. So if you're going to carry something concealed, you should know that it has to be small, flat, under loose clothing, streamlined to prevent tangling with the clothes, and in a specially made sheath and rig. If you do this, you can go to the opera without scaring people.

Chapter Ten

Fighting

Those who know how to win are far more numerous than those who know how to make proper use of their victories.
Polybius

I knew I had been out in the borderlands too long when I was sitting on Hollywood Boulevard watching a gang fight and laughing my ass off. Two Mexican gangs, evidently about four cars worth, had squared off in the middle of the street and were going at it. What made it so funny was one side would make a half-hearted charge and the other side would back down for a bit, then realize that if they were pushed too far back they'd leave their car there, so they would stop and rally. When this happened, the attacking side began to lose interest. With loss of interest the side that had been retreating would muster enough courage to form a charge. When they charged, the former attackers would begin to retreat. They'd retreat to a point until they realized if they were pushed too far back they'd lose their car. And on it went.

Every now and then they'd fuck up and charge at the same time. When this happened, about thirty seconds of fighting would ensue until they both retreated to start the shuffle all over again. This went on for about five minutes with about four real bouts of fighting.

During one of these bouts this gorilla of a guy lumbered forward with his paws outstretched, obviously ready to mangle anyone he caught. I mean this guy was big! Anyway, the gorilla lumbered towards this little guy with a tire iron. The little guy scuttled up and swung the iron at the gorilla's head. Bap, the gorilla paws at it, knocking it to the side. The fact is, the gorilla had his arms stretched out at shoulder level, making it real easy to block the swing. I'm sitting there checking off other easier targets to aim at—kidneys, balls, and knees for starters—when the little guy swings at the gorilla's head again with the same result. During the whole episode the gorilla continued to lumber forward arms outstretched. It was here that I started laughing. The little guy swung four times at the same spot and finally connected on the last one. The gorilla sagged to his knees and two of his friends dragged him to safety.

The two sides shuffled back and forth for a bit while the gorilla managed to chase down his one wit (two would imply wits). He was ready for another bout in no time and he up and lumbers forward again. Guess what? Arms held at shoulder level stretched out to grab and maul somebody. He lumbered up to a different guy who was skittering around like a chicken with a treble hook up its ass. The thing is, the dancing rooster had a knife instead of a tire iron. Gorilla lumbered up to this guy, who in turn skittered up, then back, then up, then back again. On the third advance, he got his courage up and slipped the gorilla's guard long enough to stick him in the gut. Then he skittered all the way back to his car. The gorilla took about two steps, stopped in puzzlement, reached down with a hand, turned, and walked over and sat down on the curb. I was laughing at this guy who just got stabbed because it was so pointless.

It was about that time that one side decided to pull out a shotgun and start waving it around. I dropped behind a car and watched over the hood, wondering if the thing was loaded. (To this day I think not. The guy waved it around for about thirty seconds and didn't even fire into the other gang's car. It's hard to deny that you were in a place where shots were fired when your back window is blown out and glass is everywhere.) Anyway, gorilla was still sitting there as his gang split up the road, leaving both their car and their wounded. It was at this time that the sirens could be heard. The group with the shotgun roared off in their cars, and I decided to get out of there myself. While being white, I'm dark enough to be mistaken for a Mexican (dark enough to be shot at by both sides during the Mexican gang wars in Venice), and the cops weren't going to be pleasant after this incident. Besides, I didn't want to talk to them anyway.

The long-winded yarn I just told you pretty much exemplifies most violence. Those two gangs probably weren't established enemies. More than likely they were just giving each other hard looks as they drove by and it escalated into full-scale stupidity where people got hurt. However, overall you can see that while there were about fifteen guys fighting, only one, possibly two, got seriously hurt. For the amount of time spent, the number of people involved, and the collective hardware present, the amount of actual damage was minimal. But the only guy who got hurt was hurt by a knife. Now, this should demonstrate the potential threat of a knife.

Let's shift our attention from the ape bleeding quietly on the street to the skittering chicken. That guy didn't really want to be there. Nobody else did either. They were all waiting for an excuse to get the hell out of there. The shotgun and the police were good excuses. Truth is, that guy was really pathetic with a knife. The dude he stabbed had already proved his intelligence and skill by getting his toupee rearranged with a tire iron. What do you think the skitterer's reaction would have been if he had gone up against a guy who suddenly produced a knife as well? Right; if not straight out backpedaling, a few slashes aimed at the body from a range where the only possible targets would be the arms *if* the other guy was in a Hollywood stance.

This is the reality of most knife fighting. Do not, however, confuse this with knife combat. It's incredible the amount of dick wagging that goes on with knives. Knowing this will probably not only save your life but keep you out of prison.

This is important because with this knowledge you'll be able to differentiate between a fight and a combat situation. A fight might escalate to combat status if it isn't dealt with correctly. Even though a guy got stabbed, I still call that incident a fight. If it had been combat there would have been bodies all over the place.

If you end up facing off with somebody, you need to figure out if it is really combat or only a fight, especially if the guy just pulled a knife. He may be wagging the knife around hoping that you're going to back off. If this is the case you may be able to talk him down. If he's lost control and is going mad dog, it is rapidly heading toward combat. The thing is, most incidents are not combat. If you've never seen the guy before and you both copped attitude with each other, there is no need to escalate to combat.

Many muggings are not combat situations, believe it or not. If the guy shows up and tries to roll you, you can change his mind by drawing your knife and falling into your stance. The idea behind most muggings is (at least from the mugger's standpoint) not to get hurt. Muggers are prone to suddenly remember they have to be somewhere else when they discover you're armed, too. This is the walk-up-to-you-and-say-something type of mugging, not the jump out of the bushes type. With those fuckers you go full combat mode and leave them where they fall. They deserve no quarter because they offered you none.

*   *   *   *   *

There are a few generalities about knife fighting that I'd like to talk about that I never quite got around to earlier. Therefore I'm going to stick them here instead of in the next chapter.

Targeting
There are a lot of books about what to cut off of somebody during a knife fight. In reality, you may have to deal with

a seriously reduced target area during a knife fight. A leather or denim jacket acts like light armor. Jeans do the same thing, as do high boots. Now, to make things more complicated, the area you're aiming at is not stationary. This calls for some target practice on your part. I want to point out some things you can work on to improve your targeting. These and lots of practice will get you to a point where your targeting is pretty damn good. (It took me years to get this good, but in my much-lauded heyday I used to be able to put a blade in an eye-sized target at a dead run. With that kind of speed and accuracy, who needs to be big?)

The first thing to do is to put up those little round colored stickers at various levels and in various rooms around your house. As you walk along over the next few weeks, poke your fingers at them. Practice accuracy at first, then build up speed. When you get good at it, move the stickers to different locations.

Another thing you can do is practice jabbing your fingers through a chain-link fence as you are walking along. Spot one area in advance and without slowing down, jab. At first just try to get into the hole, then as you progress try not to touch the sides. Do this on different levels until you get good at it.

Whenever you're waiting for something, practice this finger poking. Find something of suitable size and poke it a few times. Do it at work, home, the movies, and so on. In time it will become real instinctive.

The next thing is try to catch flies with your hands. If that's too frustrating, go after moths until you get the hang of it, then go big game hunting. Do yourself a favor and leave bees alone.

The next step is to take a knife and practice this targeting drill. If you've done your body training, it'll be easy to adjust to the knife. Start with larger, golf-ball-size targets scattered around a target area while you stand still. When you get good at that, start shuffling around and poking as you move, picking up speed as you progress. When you get that down to where you're striking targets about eighty percent of the time, it's time to start practicing slashes.

Find a bush with light foliage. Standing in front of the bush, slash at particular leaves and knots. After you get good at the stationary slash, begin to move around, again picking up speed as you progress.

Now take something about the size of a deadbolt (a crab apple works fine) and hang it from a cord, then slash and stab at it. Unlike the stationary targets, this one has a time limit. The slashes should be no more than two seconds apart. Because of the impact, the sucker will bounce around a lot. When you get good at this, try moving around and poking at it. You will eventually become pretty damn accurate.

Get Out Fast

One of the most lethal mistakes people make in fighting in general, but knife fighting in particular, is not getting out as fast as they went in. If you don't, your hand can get caught and you get dragged in and stabbed, or you just get your wrists slashed for you.

Options

Whenever you're up against somebody, never forget that you have more options than just your knife. Most people leave their knees open. A side kick to the knee will end a knife fight real quick. An experienced fighter will use this against you if you don't pay attention.

Shoulders

In general, when in a fight watch the guy's shoulders. Most people don't realize how much they broadcast their intentions from this part of their body.

Unknown Techniques

Most importantly, if you encounter something that you've never seen before, *get the fuck out of there!* Don't hang around to find out how the son of a bitch is going to cut you. Backpedal!

Use The Whole Knife

Never, ever forget that there are more ways to attack with a knife than just the edge. A good knife fighter will use the tip, back edge, handle, and butt against you. He can and will rip you with the tip, slash you with the back edge, either slice, gouge, or punch and have a yawara stick in his fist, or bean you with the butt.

Counters

Counters are especially common in knife fighting. If you lunge at someone, he really doesn't have to block at all. He can just flick his knife up and let you peel your arm on it. This is especially effective against people who are out of balance when they attack. There's no way they can stop in time. If they move their arm out of the way to save it, they leave themselves wide open for impromptu surgery.

Weapon Etiquette

Weapon etiquette is absolutely important when dealing with knives. Most people don't realize that a man's personal weapon is as much a part of him as his dick. Not respecting other people's weapons is a serious offense. To earn this respect for yourself, you must respect other people's weapons.

The first rule is to *never, ever* touch somebody else's knife without asking. I don't know why, but it happens quite often. When you get used to carrying a knife you'll understand. It's damn near the same thing as someone walking up and grabbing your crotch with no warning. It's really a personal insult.

The way to remember this rule is to do it yourself. If you begin to ask before you pick up a knife, it starts the trend towards respect. Another point, especially with historic knives, is after looking at the sheath, ask if you can draw it. This may seem persnickity about manners, but just remember that an armed society is a polite society. All the rude fuckers are dead.

When you hand somebody a knife, turn it inwards, point towards you. If you're nervous about it (like I am), turn the

edge out from your hand. This is an indication that you're
not attacking. Trained knife fighters don't like seeing a knife
point coming at them. Their bodies want to take over and
gut the person who is pointing it at them. With those who
are unaware, look at the knife and request they hand it to
you properly. Then quietly explain to them that it's okay but
in the future, hand over a knife hilt first. If the guy knows
better and is trying to be funny, it's hammering time. This
is not a ha-ha funny; it's something that is just not done and
anybody who thinks it's funny should be carved.

The third thing is, whenever you pull your knife for work,
tell people. As you draw say "knife" calmly and cooly. A lot
of people will freak when they suddenly notice a knife
without warning. You can even get slit because of this. You
whip a blade out without warning and there may be a few
other knife fighters around who might get uneasy about it.
In this case, uneasy may mean drawing their own knives.
Then what are you going to do?

When I have to pull my knife for work, I turn away from
people, pull the knife, and do the work out of sight of them.
This usually keeps things cool, and with knife fighting, cool
is the name of the game.

Chapter Eleven

▼

Combat

Not another one. I'm tired of having friends die.
Me, whispering, while being
held by my lady, Tracy, after
being told of a friend's death.

The reason I write my books is so maybe you'll be able to learn the lesson of combat without ever having to go through it. It is not something you want to do. It is a living hell that will stay with you the rest of your life. Unless you make youself deep and strong, it will tear you apart. I speak words of steel here. Combat is not something that ends with a body on the ground.

In the first chapter I spoke of vets—people who have come through combat—and why they are the way they are. These are people who have the mark on them. They have been in situations where they had no other choice but to fight with everything they are. It is at this point that it doesn't matter if you live or die, you are going to put everything into it. In many instances, you have to accept that you are dead already, but you are not going to die on your knees begging for life. You are going to die fighting, taking the son-of-a-bitch with you. This isn't a glorious last stand. This is stone-cold murder on your part in revenge for his killing you. No noble heroes here, just two vicious, furious wild animals ripping each other to bloody bits in the dirt and mud.

This is the attitude of combat. There is no posing, posturing, or bands playing for heroics. It is out-and-out feral. It is total commitment to everything you have, past, present, and future. If you're not ready to die trying, you're not ready for combat.

I know of only two ways to get to this point. One is to be in the shit so deep that something snaps inside of you and the beast is freed. It is then that you say, "Fuck it, kill 'em all!" At that point you'd shove a shotgun up Satan's ass and pull the trigger 'cause you just don't care anymore. People who don't get to this point die real quick, especially if it's a personal attack rather than a general one. You can choke once in a firefight and still survive if you're part of a team because there are others covering for you. You can't do that in single combat.

The other way to get to the point of combat readiness is to leave something that you care for so much that if anybody tries to hurt it you'll kill him. Plain, simple, and no frills. You're going to off the motherfucker for trying to hurt somebody you love. This point is really understood by parents and people protecting their loved ones. This isn't the same as you thinking you have a pink slip on the souls of your loved ones. (That sort of shit leads to murder when one person leaves and the other person's little ego can't take it.) This is more along the lines of, "Dude, you're not going to kill her because we're going to be killing each other instead."

This is not a macho game. This is a mature acceptance of your death to protect a loved one. It's not bragging or hyping. It's a calm, quiet decision to sacrifice yourself in order to protect someone you love. No glory or people impressing, just reality. It's no more exciting than taking out the garbage actually. This is what I meant when I said you can get to the point of combat ready without setting the beast free. You simply have your hand on the beast's leash and know you can and will set him free to protect your loved ones.

When you are in combat many things will happen inside and outside of you. These things are important because they may affect what's going on.

There may be many things going on in your mind, but physically you will go to an extreme. This is why you must have instinctive body reactions. Your reactions have to be purely physiological. If you've trained your body, it will react correctly while your mind is screaming in total panic. Without this training, you will freeze and die.

In one sense your body overrides your mind in order to survive. Blood rushes from the outer skin inward, pooling in the stomach and muscles. This is why in many cases you don't really bleed until afterward. You will also experience trembling, tunnel vision, and possible sphincter release. Occasionally, certain muscles may lock up on you. (I've had to pry things out of my hands afterwards.) Your adrenaline level gets kicked to the moon and pain sensors get turned off. In other words, you become a total killing machine for a period of time.

In combat, your time perception is blasted one way or the other. Everything may speed up and blast by at a blur. This is really scary until you realize that your reactions have been kicked up to the same level. You move faster than normal in this state. Time can also seem slower in combat. Actually, I don't know if that's the case or if your reactions speed up to a point faster than what's happening around you. Things take a long time to occur while you're moving at super speed. I've seen the knife coming at me, twisted my whole body, and grabbed the guy's arm in such a way that I could disarm him—all in the time it took him to do half of a strike.

Afterward, aside from any injuries you've acquired, you're exhausted and sore. You get the shakes. Some people get nauseous to the point of vomiting because every nerve in their body starts screaming in bloody terror. You're jittery and quick to jump. Mentally it's just as fun. Part of you is screaming that you almost got your ass killed, while another part is reeling with repulsion, and still a third part is scared shitless. Your brain is shorting out because every nerve in your body is talking at once. Suddenly you're aware of every ache, scratch, itch, pressure, texture, and temperature. And what is totally human, but seriously frowned on by society, is you're hornier than a three-balled tomcat.

It's important to remember that this is an extreme! You do not want this to become a regular part of your programming. I know a guy who dropped out of the Rangers because he was having an orgasm every time he killed a person. He was an assassin whose specialty was knives. Fortunately, he was sane enough to recognize it really was sick. He began to back off after that.

The reality of knife combat is that you are killing people. Hollywood doesn't show what it's really about. People get shot and grab their chest and fall over. A nice, neat little bullet hole. They don't show the exit hole, which is a cavity blown out of a hunk of bloody meat that used to be a living human being. The same thing is true about knives. A quick stab and the guy falls down. Bullshit! Slice somebody in the stomach and blood and white guts will spill out all over you and the ground. Especially with knives, when it is over you're going to have blood all over you. Not only yours but your dead opponent. There is no more sickening stench than human blood. Once you've had it in your nose it never goes away. The very smell will begin to repulse you after awhile.

If you've closed with the guy, you have to hold him until he is either dead or too weak to strike back. They don't drop nice, neat, and clean like in the movies. They kick, twitch, and bleed. Another thing is if the guy's sphincter and bladder didn't let go before, they will now. So besides his blood, you're covered with piss and shit as well.

That's the other guy. Unlike what happens in the movies, he may have gotten you, too. Look down at your sliced arm hanging useless at your side pouring blood. It's numb now but the pain will come soon. If you're lucky, he didn't slash any nerves because if he did, you've just lost the use of your arm for the rest of your life. If you're lucky, you only have to go to the hospital for surgery, then spend the next six months trying to relearn how to use your arm.

If he got a body shot in, you're going to the hospital for about three weeks. It's during this time that you'd better hope he didn't have friends. They may be looking for you soon.

To top it all off, the police are going to show up and ask you some serious questions about why you did what you did. Even if they let you off the hook, you will always have the spectre hanging over you.

This is what knife fighting is really about. Not some paramilitary fantasy, but an ugly, vicious reality, a reality that will destroy you if you are not strong enough to deal with it. Despite how hideous it is, though, you might have to do it someday in an emergency situation. That's why I spent so much of this book telling you how to avoid it. Most times you will find out that violence is not a solution. How well you'll do out there depends on who you are and how fast you recognize other options. It isn't for anybody else that you must learn this; it's for you and your survival.

This chapter is really about personal responsibility. Not the bullshit strings that people use to control you, but responsibility to and for yourself. Along with this responsibility comes an understanding of things most people never even know exist. Because they don't know about them they have no concept of what real responsibility is. They think it's something you must do to serve someone else.

A lot of people think I screw around too much. I'm sure that in many ways I do. Wannabe macho men get bent out of shape by my screwing around. Well, until they get in my face, that's their problem. Mine is dealing with the ghosts who ride with me. There are times when I nearly go insane because of what is behind me. It is because of these ghosts and my past that I blow off steam the way I do. I'm laughing to ease the pain.

I have done things to survive that have marked my soul. I carry the mark of the warrior and it scares the shit out of others and even myself sometimes. When I walk into a place, people recoil because of what they sense—a person who has not only gone through something they are terrified of but would do so again if necessary. This is something that I cannot turn off; it is there and part of me. The best I can do is control it. It is not something that is "great to have." It's an awesome power and even more of an awesome responsibility. If you don't control it, it will kill you more effectively than any enemy you will ever encounter.

Some people who want this mark think it is a toy, something to scare away all of those little whip-dicks who pester you through life. Others are egomaniacs who want to lord over lesser mortals, using it as a support to their magnificence. These are the people who die or are thrown in jail because they don't understand the responsibility that comes with it. Others get there without a sufficient mental and emotional framework and are driven insane by the responsibility.

Other people, and I hope you are one, simply are afraid of being hurt and want to protect themselves. There's always the fear of, "What if I choke at the last minute?" This really is fear of "What if I'm not good enough?" It's okay to feel that way. Many other warriors understand that fear. We rode that trail and we know it well. I personally feel fear is a result of the lies our culture insists on promoting. All your life you were told to "be a man," and yet every time you tried to you got nailed for it. I used to be told to act like a man. Well, those who were saying that to me were pretty fuckin' vague as to what that meant. To me, it meant be like John Wayne and stand up for myself. Standing up for myself sometimes meant fighting. When I did, I'd get in trouble because I was supposed to stand up for myself without fighting. That's bullshit! They'd tell me not to be a coward, but not to fight either. Thanks a lot. What did they want me to do, use harsh language?

I grew up in a bad-assed neighborhood where there were two types of people: predators and food. I was neither; I was an omnivore. I didn't want to attack others, I just wanted to be left the fuck alone to do my thing. The predators came after me and I fought them. I got so good at it that I began to think I was one of them. I thought predators were strong and therefore I had to be just as strong, if not more. That's because I only saw the two extremes—if I wasn't a predator, I was food. It was during this time that I earned the warrior's mark, although at the time I didn't know it.

As the years went on I began to notice a marked difference between me and those who preyed on others. They couldn't create; they had to steal from others. I didn't need to attack others like they did. I didn't know it at the time, but most predators aren't strong, they're sneaky chickenshits. They are coyotes, not wolves.

I realized I could do other things besides fighting and destroying. I could create, which is something they couldn't do. That's what prompted the attacks in the first place. I had been creating, but now I could do it again, this time for me. They were still there, the predators, and they were still attacking each other. I was strong enough that the predators couldn't take away the things I had made. They were mine and nobody was going to take them away.

This is what motivated me to walk the Warrior's Path. What is bringing you to this path may be entirely different. Whatever your reasons, you are here now. It is from this point that I will give you the greatest gift of wisdom I know to avoid the mistakes that I have made in my life. That is, *grow inside*. Let your own roots, not somebody else's, go deep within you. Discover who you really are, not who the coyotes say you are so they can steal from you. You need to find your own definition of yourself. If you need to you can rise to fight, but you are much more than just a mere fighter and no motherfucker is ever going to take that away from you. Remember this motto: "I am here, and this is me. You can kill me, but nobody can destroy me." This will scare away most of the coyotes and make the rest real hesitant about fucking with you for no reason. When you reach this point, then you are a warrior.

▼

Afterword

Whaddya want? A blowjob?!
Me, snarling at somebody
who was sniveling about
something trivial.

In case you haven't noticed, there are better things you can do with your time than knife fighting. Unfortunately, life can be somewhat of a bitch and force things on you that you really don't want. Just remember that there is always more than one way to skin a cat. I've tried to show you some of the things you can do to keep from killing someone unnecessarily, and to tell you what you should know before you get into a knife fight. Being in the middle of a knife fight is no time to discover what can go wrong. The reason most people get hurt is because they didn't know this stuff and it blew up in their faces.

The last chapter was a real bitch for me to write. It stirred up some demons that I thought I had long since laid to rest. One of the main reasons I write these books—aside from purely mercenary motives—is because I wish someone had told me these things when I was there. The many teachers, friends, and comrades that I rode with over the years taught me many of these things, but I paid blood lessons for many more. I understand the feelings of people who read these kinds of books; I was there myself. It's something you have to do, and it is a valid path.

In many ways I am an outlaw. Because I rode some hard trails I can never walk in certain social circles comfortably. They sense my mark and are uneasy. When I was younger I used to think it was great to scare those assholes. But ten or so years of carrying that mark has left me a different man.

Because I could never walk in some circles, I went further into the borderlands. In many ways those lands are wild and vicious, but as I traveled I discovered exactly how big the world really is. What's more, I discovered that I could be happy out there. I didn't have to stay in limited circles. In time I became just as much of an explorer/adventurer as a warrior.

To survive in the borderlands you have to leave your definitions behind. You'd be amazed at what you can learn by keeping your eyes and mind open. It also can be funner 'n shit out there. As I look back at those circles now, I feel more pity than anything else for them. They are locked in one tiny world they can never escape. What's worse is most of them aren't happy about being there. Yet their fear makes it so they can't leave. Look and see how many people are drinking and drugging themselves to death because they're trapped in a limited world. Because I know how to take care of myself, I can go anywhere. And to tell you the truth, I'm having a good time and am happier 'n a pig in shit.

I've tried to share with you the fact that sometimes you have to fight, even kill. If you survive, you can discover things that you never dreamed of beyond that point. And now that you can take care of yourself, you are qualified to get there. The Warriors' Way is a path, not a destination. Just remember:

Fuck it! Have fun while exploring!

About the Author

Born sometime when he "was sorta' young," Marc "Animal" MacYoung began life on the proper footing: he pissed on the doctor in revenge for getting hit. His first word was not "momma" or "dada," but a four letter expletive referring to the act of copulation. He has held a steady course in life ever since.

Fortunately for the rest of the country, he is still terrorizing Los Angeles. As long as he stays there, women, sheep, and beer in the rest of the United States will remain safe. (Although, for reasons best not speculated on, he has been learning American Indian Sign Language.)

At this time, his lady, Tracy, hasn't strangled him yet, which is a good sign. Animal claims the reason she can handle him is that she grew up with a mountain lion as a playmate and de facto mother. This seems like a reasonable qualification for being able to put up with him for any length of time.